NAMES AND NAMING IN JOYCE

Names and Naming
in Joyce

Claire A. Culleton

THE UNIVERSITY OF WISCONSIN PRESS

The University of Wisconsin Press
114 North Murray Street
Madison, Wisconsin 53715

3 Henrietta Street
London WC2E 8LU, England

Library of Congress Cataloging-in-Publication Data
Culleton, Claire A.
Names and naming in Joyce / Claire A. Culleton.
160 p.   cm.
Includes bibliographical references (p.) and index:
ISBN 0-299-14380-5   ISBN 0-299-14384-8 (pbk.)
1. Joyce, James, 1882–1941—Knowledge—Onomastics.
2. Characters and characteristics in literature.
3. Joyce, James, 1882–1941—Characters.
4. Names, Personal, in literature.
5. Names, Irish, in literature.
6. Onomastics in literature.   I. Title.
PR6019.09Z5278   1994
823'.912—dc20   94-15380

For Kiki and Carole, and
for Jake's daughters everywhere

CONTENTS

Acknowledgments   ix
Abbreviations   xi

Introduction   3
1. Naming and Allusion in Joyce   8
2. Naming and History   43
3. Naming and Gender   72
4. Naming, Nameplay, and Revenge   95
5. Naming and Identity   109

Notes   129
Works Cited   135
Index   142

ACKNOWLEDGMENTS

Sincere and heartfelt thanks to Berni Benstock, Shari Benstock, Zack Bowen, and Patrick McCarthy of the University of Miami; John Bishop of the University of California at Berkeley; Phillip Herring of the University of Wisconsin–Madison; John Nagle of Manhattan College; Dick Penner of the University of Tennessee; Stephen Watt of Indiana University; Henry Logan, Bob and Lakshmi McGrath, Adrian Peever, and John and Ileana Slack of the Miami *Wake* group; the Kent *Wake* group, DYOUBLONG?; my colleagues at Kent State University; the Kent State University Research Council; Esim Erdim, Ted Fullerton, Amy Cronauer, Nick Traenkner, and Carol O'Keefe; the staff of the University of Wisconsin Press, especially its director, Allen Fitchen, and Raphael Kadushin and Diana Cook; my family and friends, especially Mom, Kiki, Carole, Chris, Suleica, and Tom; the Slatterys (London, Dublin, Thurles, Portlaoise); Belinda Ghitis, Rocco Marinaccio, Karah Stokes, and Kathryn Swain; and my students, past and present, who aren't afraid to be passionate about literature, especially Lorie Hershberger, Carol O'Keefe, and Steve Wilson.

Sections of chapters 2 and 3 of this book have been published in slightly different forms as "Patronymics and Onomastics in Joyce's 'Oxen of the Sun' " (*Onomastica Canadiana* 70.1 [1988]: 23–32) and "Naming and Gender in James Joyce's Fiction" (*Names: The Journal of the American Name Society* 39.4 [1991]: 303–18). I am grateful to the editors of *Onomastica Canadiana* and *Names* for permission to reprint these essays. Moreover, I gratefully acknowledge permission to quote from Oliver Gogarty's unpublished letters, Cornell University Library, Rare and Manuscript Collections.

ABBREVIATIONS

All references made to the works listed in Works Cited are given parenthetically. References to Joyce's works are abbreviated and cited parenthetically. References to *Ulysses* are cited by chapter and line number; references to *Finnegans Wake* are cited with page and line numbers; references to *Letters* are cited with volume and page number. The following standard abbreviations have been adopted:

D	*Dubliners.* 1914. New York: Penguin Books, 1982.
E	*Exiles.* 1918. London: Penguin Books, 1979.
FW	*Finnegans Wake.* 1939. New York: Penguin Books, 1982.
GJ	*Giacomo Joyce.* 1914. London: Faber and Faber, 1968.
Letters 1, 2, 3	*Letters of James Joyce.* Vol. 1, edited by Stuart Gilbert, New York: Viking Press, 1957; reissued with corrections, 1965. Vols. 2 and 3, edited by Richard Ellmann, New York: Viking Press, 1966.
P	*A Portrait of the Artist as a Young Man.* 1916. New York: Penguin Books, 1982.
SH	*Stephen Hero.* 1905. Edited by John J. Slocum and Herbert Cahoon, New York: New Directions, 1944, 1963.
SL	*Selected Letters.* Edited by Richard Ellmann. New York: Viking Press, 1975.
U	*Ulysses.* 1922. The corrected text, edited by Hans Walter Gabler. New York: Random House, 1986.

NAMES AND NAMING IN JOYCE

Introduction

On the very first page of the very first work of fiction that James Joyce published, the first character we meet admits a long-time fascination with the word *gnomon* (*D* 9). It is appropriate and perhaps no coincidence that the hypnotic word *gnomon* is a homonym of the Latin *nomen*, name, particularly since the boy himself is unnamed, and especially since the unnamed boy soon becomes a namer in "An Encounter" where he says to his friend Mahony, "Let you be Murphy and I'll be Smith" (*D* 26). The homophonic association of *gnomon* and *nomen* is strengthened when it appears recycled later in *Finnegan's Wake*, where Joyce puns on the two words, saying that HCE was known "by the mnames of . . . gnomeosulphidosalamermauderman" (*FW* 595.34–596.14), the silent *m* of *mnames* mimicking the silent *g* in *gnomon*, while the initial *gnomeo* of the neologism puns on the triumvirate of *gnomon*, *nomen*, and Romeo. The Romeo allusion in this particular instance is most likely a reference to Juliet's apostrophe, "What's in a name?" since the pun suggests all three possibilities. The Latin *nomen* is also used in *Finnegans Wake* where Joyce adds an *-ed* to its ending, punning, again, on the English word *named*: "an engles to the teeth who, no-mened Nash of Girahash, would go anyold where" (*FW* 75.31–32).[1] Apart from these and other references where Joyce puns on *name*, *nomen*, and *gnomon*, Joyce also indicates the importance of names when, in the *Wake*, the name of his alter ego is the Hebrew word for *name*: *shem*. In Hebrew studies, one rarely sees written the name of God—only *shemoth*, name substitutes. Shem's allusive, Hebraic name, aligned by association with the names for God, is important, since Shem is both the artist figure and creator in *Finnegans Wake*. Moreover, the Talmud informs readers that "a man is said to have created life by reciting names" (Ashley *What's in a Name?* 216); thus, the link between naming, power, and creation is an essential one in understanding Joyce—and he clues us in about the importance of names from the very first page of *Dubliners,* where the *gnomon/nomen* association is suggested, to the very last paragraph of *Finnegans Wake,* where Anna Livia Plurabelle, rechristened *allaniuvia pulchrabelled* (FW 627.27–28), thinks to herself, "Auravoles, they says, never heed of your name!" (*FW* 627.32–33). The names, the *shemoth,* the nominal play that resound throughout Joyce's canon invite attention. Unnamed, named, and re-named, characters in Joyce's works often assume a variety of nominal markers, and a knowledge of the genealogies of the names Joyce uses in his works, as well as their truncations, misspellings, duplications, and comic juxtapositionings, can inform and substantially enhance the reading of Joyce's texts, since Joyce's names are never gratuitous and each is tied in some way to his complex and eclectic allusive method.

The narrator's fascination in *Dubliners* with *gnomon* seems an early indication that names are pointers, indicators, shadows that can be used as interpreters—and, like the Euclidean gnomon referred to by the young narrator, names can be broken down into distinct units, each a representation, a shadow, of the whole. Studying names in Joyce we not only find largely untapped resources that extend our study of gene-alogy, history, sociology, folklore, literature, philosophy, and other dis-ciplines outside of linguistics, but we enhance our ultimate understand-ing of the writer with whatever information we can harness about the processes Joyce went through when he selected names for his charac-ters. More important, understanding how names work in Joyce aids our understanding of Joyce's complex psychology of invention and his intricate and allusive composition process, something readers and crit-ics alike have been trying to pin down for years.[2]

This study is not an annotated catalogue of names—fine work has been done in this area by Adaline Glasheen and by Shari Benstock and Bernard Benstock;[3] nor is this a junket into the dramatis personae of Joyce's works. Instead, this is a theoretical and conceptual study of onomastics in Joyce, focusing on a number of areas: naming and allu-sion, naming and history, naming and gender, naming and magic and the occult, naming and sexuality, naming and identity, and naming and revenge as they pertain to Joyce's canon. Journalists often repeat with amusement the story of a television reporter whom Jacqueline Ken-nedy was showing around the redecorated White House. Camera crews following behind him, the reporter asked Jacqueline Kennedy if she would mind pointing out some of the pictures to them. "Certainly," she replied. "There's a picture, and there's a picture, and there's another picture over there" (Ashley *What's in a Name?* 199). It would be easy to take a look at some of the names sprinkled throughout Joyce's books, calling attention to the puns, the playfulness, the perversities embedded in each; but more work needs to be done to help us understand how the names function, how they work aesthetically, how they both disguise and reveal Joyce's allusive method. Because Joyce was so interested in names, we can learn a lot from the way he selects character names. Critics have wrestled for decades about what it is that governs Joyce's literary selection, what principles inform his heteroglossic creative process. Names hold many clues, and they're a fascinating place to start, since they raise exciting issues and can help redesign our approach to Joyce, energizing our readings of his familiar texts.

We know that Joyce was a superstitious man, often calling attention to what he thought were talismanic coincidences, such as the publication dates of his books, as the following letter to Harriet Weaver suggests:

> A coincidence is that of birthdays in connection with my books. *A Portrait of the Artist* which first appeared serially in your paper on 2 February [Joyce's birthday] finished on 1 September [Weaver's birthday]. *Ulysses* began on 1 March (birthday of a friend of mine, a Cornish painter [Budgen]) and was finished on Mr Pound's birthday, he tells me. I wonder on whose it will be published. (*Letters* 3:52)

Joyce also exhibited a certain superstition about names in his letters. In his letters to Nora where he asked about her relationship with Cosgrave, for example, Joyce only referred to Cosgrave as "that other," never by name (Maddox *Nora* 91). Another indication of Joyce's superstition is that he would not sign his name if the letter imported estrangement, or if it were heavily apologetic, as in this 18 November 1909 letter to Nora:

> [no salutation] I dare not address you tonight by any familiar name. . . .
> Nora, remember something good of the poor wretch who dishonoured you with his love. Think that your lips have kissed him and your hair has fallen over him and that your arms have held him to you.
> I will not sign my name because it is the name you called me when you loved me and honoured me and gave me your young tender soul to wound and betray. (*SL* 177–78)

Brenda Maddox notes that Joyce attached particular taboos to the use of his first name, and that even though he was able to greet Nora as "Little Pouting Nora" in a letter of 8 July 1904 he signed that letter only with his initials, J. A. J. (31). Maddox adds,

> Even when he told her that he was becoming closer to her than to anyone he knew because when he was with her he dropped his usual cynicism, he could not decide what to sign himself and so he did not sign anything at all. Sometimes he hid behind fey pseudonyms. . . . It was September before he could bring himself to write "Jim." (31)

Of course, Joyce's relationship to names was not only one of awe or fear; he also played with names in his letters, addressing Harriet Weaver, for example, as "t.r.," the last letters of her first and last names, in response to a letter she signed backward—"Revaew Teirrah"—on 3 December 1926 (*Letters* 3:147–48). He also feared the coincidence that Homer's name meant blindness, since he, too, was struggling with the same illness that afflicted the Greek poet; but he counteracted that strange coincidence with another, noting with fortuity that his editor, like Homer's Penelope, was a weaver, extracting as his letters indicate amusement—and consolation—from Weaver's name. The nominal play evidenced in Joyce's letters is amplified in his fiction and given serious attention in his writings. Joyce often was guided by names and their associations, and he contemplated the magical value of names, negotiating the significance of them to his life and to his art.

When Joyce proposed that the writer James Stephens finish the *Wake*, for example, not only was he guided by his enjoyment over their shared birthday, but he contemplated, as well, "the aesthetic value [that] their combined initials, *J J and S*" would bring to the title page (Borodin 155), a reference to the famed Irish distillers John Jameson and Sons. Glasheen notes in the *Third Census of "Finnegans Wake"* that Joyce was attracted to the Jameson distillery because it transformed the water of the Liffey—"mud and all," Joyce wrote—into whiskey, imitating his own office by taking natural substance and transforming it into art (142). The serendipity of the initials, then, was not only fortuitous but magical to the superstitious Joyce.

In his published letters Joyce reveals a keen interest in names, what we might even call a faith in names, in their powers and in their possibilities, in their potential and in their portentousness. Like his letters,

Joyce's fiction resounds with onomastic consequence, not only teeming with what many readers see as his nominal play but fertile with indications of the importance of names and naming. Engaged and fascinated with names, Joyce inscribed in his works his onomastic curiosity, and an examination of the names, their functions, their origins, their pluralities, and their exploitable suggestiveness remains essential to our understanding of Joyce and his writings. Both serious and playful, discerning and disconcerting, Joyce's onomastic bravado becomes an element tied to his aesthetics, one that is grounded in the Irish literary tradition of magic, creation, power, and rhetorical one-upmanship. In the literary text, the functions of and the relationships between names become understandably exaggerated, since authors often exploit the connections between a character and his or her name; but when the text itself is a metaphor and a vehicle for exaggeration—as some might argue of *Finnegans Wake*, for example—the processes and patterns of naming warrant explicit investigation. To be sure, naming always carries with it considerations of history, politics, gender, and literary consequence; and Joyce's canon provides a practical means of investigating the symbiotic ties among the four.

CHAPTER ONE

Naming and Allusion in Joyce

When Stephen Dedalus says in the Scylla and Charybdis episode of *Ulysses* that Shakespeare "had a good groatsworth of wit . . . and no truant memory," adding that Shakespeare "carried a memory in his wallet" (*U* 9.245–46), his assessment of Shakespeare's talent sets up for the student of Joyce the polarities inherent in Joyce's allusive method and the artistic tensions between the two: invention and memory. If an artist has "no truant memory," and can recall with gleaned accuracy parts of a text, going through the throes of inspiration even while trying to repeat lines and phrases written by another artist or poet, should he be praised or made suspect when he incorporates those texts into his own? If he discounts authorial allegiance, violating literary property at every turn imaginable, as Joyce does, do his literary allusions become more than allusions? What sort of methodology does Joyce adopt, what principles govern his literary appropriation, and how do his naming practices illuminate his unique methods of allusion?

We get an idea of Joyce's allusive method from Stephen. Stephen's multiple allusions in *Ulysses* to Robert Greene's *Groatsworth of Witte*[1] (1592) are important to our understanding of Joyce's allusive method, since Greene's *Groatsworth* contains the earliest discussion of Shakespeare's methodology. Although scholars agree that Greene's *Groatsworth* is not a remarkable piece of literature, they find the short work valuable for the information it provides scholars about the workings, the schemata, and the labor hierarchy that characterized the Elizabethan and Jacobean stage. The last few pages of *Groatsworth* are particularly valuable and familiar because they contain not only the dying playwright's advice to his stage contemporaries Marlowe, Peele, and Nashe but also the earliest allusion to William Shakespeare, and they indicate that Shakespeare was in London in 1592 and successful—a fact not generally accepted until Thomas Tyrwhitt in 1766 identified the "upstart Crow" passage in *Groatsworth* as a reference to Shakespeare:

> There is an upstart Crow, beautified with our feathers, that with his *tigers heart wrapped in a player's hide* supposes he is as well able to bombast out a blank verse as the best of you: and being an absolute *Johannes-factotum* is in his own conceit the only Shake-scene in a country. (Greene 46)

Greene's reference to Shakespeare as an "upstart Crow, beautified with our feathers," calls into question Shakespeare's originality, and the allusion continues to prompt debate over the primary authorship of some of Shakespeare's plays. Greene's pun on Shakespeare's name, where he alludes to the author's conceit in assuming that he is the "only Shake-scene in a country," is a reference repeated by Stephen in Scylla and Charybdis (*U* 9.926–27), and a pun not unlike Shakespeare's own rendering of his coat of arms.[2] Yet the references to *Groatsworth of Witte* in *Ulysses* yield more than allusory parallels to the Elizabethan age, since they delineate or establish the two camps of Joyce's rhetoric of imitation, that of invention and that of memory.

Greene's grievance regarding Shakespeare is that the playwright rose to fame by stealing his literary material from contemporary playwrights such as Greene himself, Marlowe, Peele, and Nashe. Pointing out that Shakespeare was originally an actor who, like a "burr" (Greene 47), stuck to these playwrights for fame, Greene claims that when Shakespeare began to write his own plays, he borrowed from the invention of his contemporaries and predecessors. Greene's *Groatsworth*, then, raises the questions of primary invention and artistic protocol, and attacks Shakespeare on both counts.

Importantly, Shakespeare was most likely aware of Greene's attack in 1592, since he referred to it some years later in *Hamlet*. When Polonius reads to the Queen a letter he probably forged to Ophelia from the Prince, Polonius comments on the word *beautified* contained in the letter, saying "That's an ill phrase, a vile phrase; 'beautified' is a vile phrase" (*Hamlet* 2.2.110–12). Shakespeare's self-conscious reference to Greene's charges indicates not only his contempt for the allegation, calling attention simultaneously to his vilification of the indictment and of the language, but also Shakespeare's bravado, since he specifically uses the word here, in a presumably forged document. The gesture is full of good humor, too, since Shakespeare is comically appropriating the words of a critic who faulted him for appropriating the words of others.

Joyce's multiple allusions in *Ulysses* to Greene's *Groatsworth* lead us to a source laden with extra-textual significance, and may indicate Joyce's own concern over the issue of primary invention, or his anxieties about lacking it. Leopold Bloom, for example, uses the word *beautify* moments before Lenehan charges him with plagiarism in Circe (*U* 15.1667; 15.1734). And when Joyce uses the word again in the Lessons chapter of *Finnegans Wake*, he merges the term *beautified* with *beatified*, creating *beautifed* (*FW* 262.n6), a neologism suggesting that literary appropriation and allusive embellishment are venues to canonization, indicating as well that he has beautified his own prose by feeding off the invention of others.

To be sure, when we first meet Stephen in *Ulysses*, he is not very mindful of authorial property: his most notable sayings are plagiarized from Wilde, "cribbed out of Meredith" (*U* 14.1486), informed by Shakespeare, and influenced by his consubstantial father's voice; his mind is filled with overwrought allusions and teems with quotations; the Goulding vignette he creates early in the Proteus episode borrows its language from a number of sources, a polyphonic vignette beautified with Elizabethan English and the characteristic utterances of his father, Simon; moreover, what we see of the pale vampire poem Stephen creates toward the end of that episode echoes Douglas Hyde's poem "My Grief on the Sea." Changing the very concept of literary allusion from something once used to ornament and decorate a literary piece to something that augments themes in his works, pointing to references outside the text that enlarge our understanding of particular passages, Joyce often tests the boundaries of allusion. While Joyce's literary and historical allusions often extend our understanding of the plot, or aid our understanding of his characters and their thoughts, the names he selects for his characters, his pubs, his streets, his churches, and other geographical landmarks often raise and answer at the same time questions about Joyce's complex matrix of allusion, and his intricate and obscure allusive method.

Though Joyce never explained his allusive method, indicating how or why he amplified his texts with allusive fragments, he did criticize the allusions of others. Joyce complained in a letter to his brother Stanislaus, for example, that Oscar Wilde's *Picture of Dorian Gray* made little use of what few allusions it contained, saying, "If [Wilde] had had the courage to develop the allusions in the book it might have been better" (*Letters* 2:150). Joyce's comment is an interesting one because he refers to Wilde's allusions to homosexuality in the book—allusions that are draped themselves in literary and historical allusion. Stanislaus writes in *My Brother's Keeper* of a similar instance, when Joyce disapproved of an allusive title on an essay by Oliver Gogarty; Joyce's complaint was that Gogarty's essay was not good enough to warrant the allusion. Stanislaus explains:

> As regards work he was at a loose end, and, probably acting on Yeats's suggestion, asked me to give him some titles for essays. I made out a list of half a dozen or so, . . . Revellers, Athletic Beauty, A Portrait of the Artist . . . 'Contra Gentiles'. . . . Nothing came of it for the moment; he wrote no essay then, but he spoke to Gogarty of his intention to write an essay and call it *Contra Gentiles*. A short time afterwards Gogarty produced an essay with that title, and showed it to my brother. Jim read the essay, and then turned down and creased and neatly tore off the top of the page that bore the title. Gogarty pooh-poohed the gesture, and made some rambling statement about 'all of us using the same alphabet'.
>   I asked Jim why he had torn the title off.
>   —After all, said I, if Gogarty borrowed the title, it wasn't yours either.
>   —I did not tear it off because he borrowed it, said Jim, I tore it off because he wasted it. What he had written was all nonsense. (242–43).

No doubt, Gogarty's remark about "all of us using the same alphabet" was a fortuitous comment, and one that most likely was not lost on Joyce; but Joyce's response to his brother's logic indicates that he believed that allusion was a serious business, that a writer had an obligation to use allusion "properly" and to his best literary advantage, squeezing as much from the reference as possible, a concept that Lewis Carroll's Humpty Dumpty articulated decades before when he told Alice, "When I make a word do a lot of work like that, . . . I always pay it extra" (214). Names in Joyce, like Humpty Dumpty's overworked words, put in lots of double hours, often extending the allusive field in many directions, as we shall see, often corroborating the allusiveness of another name in the text while at the same time suggesting their own, autonomously.

The allusiveness of Kathleen Kearney's name, for example, the musical daughter in Joyce's short story "A Mother," is extended when Joyce introduces the character Hoppy Holohan. Mrs. Kearney, we are told, decided she would take advantage of her daughter's name, *Kathleen*, since it had become a popular name among her friends at the Eire Abu Society. Because the name *Kathleen* in this context suggests *Kathleen ni Houlihan*, the *Holohan* reference extends the allusiveness of *Kathleen*, since *Holohan* strengthens Kathleen Kearney's ironic association with Kathleen ni Houlihan, and forms between the names of the two characters an intricate web of reference that extends beyond the frame of the page. The same can be said of the name *Sinico:* the appearance of the name *"Captain" Sinico* in a story that borders on adulterous themes might well suggest to readers the Captain O'Shea/Kitty O'Shea/Parnell triangle, especially since Joyce encodes the word *sin* in the first syllable of the Sinico name.

Names often act as supplemental allusions in Joyce's texts, allusions that augment Joyce's themes; yet they exist just as independently and function just as critically as other allusions do—the literary, the historical, the criminal, the theological, and the scientific, for example. Allusions in Joyce are much like the notes jotted in Joyce's notesheets in that they are "shorthand" memos intended to remind us in capsule form of the full context from which the reference is drawn. Many of Joyce's allusions act as "pointers," gnomons that refer the reader to a passage in a text that has more significance to the passage we are reading than that which is cited by Joyce; and the unarticularted parallels between the two texts are often more interesting and appropriate when fully explored or drawn out than they are in the encapsulated version introduced and suggested in Joyce's text by a word, a phrase, a title, a name. Joyce's multiple allusions do not merely amplify themes but point, instead, to that which needs outside explanation, inviting the reader not only to identify the source, but to "interpret the technique of allusion itself" (Riquelme 1). Joyce's layering of references accounts, in part, for the uniqueness of his allusive method, and his layering and texturing of allusion, specifically his nominal play, extend the scope of his fiction onto many linguistic battlefields.

Because of its allusiveness, *Ulysses* calls attention to its own derivativeness, an aspect of Modernist art that has been referred to as self-exposing plagiarism (Lawrence 237), since in *Ulysses* Joyce often displays and announces his sources. The sources most impressive to Joyce the reader, to Joyce the writer, surface in subtle or exaggerated forms in Joyce's texts. Like Shakespeare, Joyce had "no truant memory" (*U* 9.245); what he read he retained both in memorized and ameliorated forms, incorporating much of his own reading into his texts, reinforcing and resounding literary invention with literary association, often just as "covetous of his neighbour's word" as Shem the Penman (*FW* 172.30).

Shem, Shaun divulges in chapter 7 of *Finnegans Wake*, writes in a "murderous mirrorhand," claiming that he is "aware of no other shaggspick, other Shakhisbeard, either prexactly . . . or procisely the seem as . . . what he fancied or guessed . . . he was himself" (*FW* 177.31–35); yet his literary ignorance is not only an arguable posture but a self-effacing one. Joyce's characteristic "mirrorhand," his self-exposing plagiarism, his literary appropriation, what Eliot would call his "making better,"[3] is what is so intriguing about Joyce's allusive method. His layering and texturing of the mirrored prose invite inspection and definition, challenging all the while our assumptions about what constitutes an original text.

Lewis Carroll wrote in his "Preface" to *Sylvie and Bruno*, a book Joyce probably read in 1927,[4] that "perhaps the hardest thing in all literature—at least *I* have found it so: by no voluntary effort can I accomplish it: I have to take it as it comes—is to write anything *original*" (279). Whether Joyce conceived of originality as an intentional and voluntary act, or even as a desirable act, for that matter, remains arguable; indeed, after Stephen listens to Bloom describe in Ithaca his idea for an advertisement, Stephen deduces that "originality, though producing its own reward, does not invariably conduce to success" (*U* 17.606–7). It is important to understand how Joyce appropriates the originality of others, integrates it with his own, and forges their genius of inspiration onto his own literary inventions.

What is Joyce's allusive method, and how is his method manifested in his choice of character names? In what ways can we trace, outline, or gauge Joyce's own derivative reading and writing in his naming, and how can this help us understand his methodology? Paul Gauguin once remarked that every artist is either a plagiarist or a revolutionary. What Joyce reveals about his allusive method through his use of names and naming is that clearly he is both. The distinctive naming habits and patterns that he developed over the years can be revealing, since his onomastic "routine" helps us to understand and anticipate his onomastic manipulations and intentions. Those patterns characteristic of Joyce's writings, those certain forms into which Joyce's literary onomastics falls, the literary associations and the literary correspondences, and

the aesthetic and literary contexts of the names he selects for his characters, contain significant information about the workings of Joyce's allusive method and, as such, are essential documents in our effort to understand his creative process.

A number of component elements can be identified as they relate
specifically to Joyce's naming practices. Among these is his attempt at
verisimilitude. Joyce endows his texts with real names of real Dubliners, names from the society evoked in his works. In his attempts at
verisimilitude, Joyce inscribes in his works character names of Dublin
residents taken, for example, from *Thom's Directory*, the "tellafun book"
probably noted in *Finnegans Wake* out of which Crowbar and Festy King
select the "illassumed names" Tykingfest and Rabworc (*FW* 86.13).
This particular kind of backward nameplay is an onomastic technique
often found in Joyce—we've already seen how he made use of it in his
letters to Harriet Weaver—but the backward naming becomes especially significant in *Finnegans Wake*, as we shall see, since it frustrates
the linearity of the text.

Though verisimilitude was one of Joyce's governing principles, not
every name in Joyce's texts is traceable to a living person; but Joyce was
careful to people his texts with names that maintained the nominal in-
tegrity of his works, making sure to use names that were acceptably
Irish, names that believably fit the milieu of Dublin during the particular era in which his work was set. Richard Ellmann notes that "the verisimilitude in *Ulysses* is so compelling that Joyce has been derided as
more mimic than creator, which charge, being untrue, is the greatest
praise of all" (363). To preserve the cultural veracity of his fiction, Joyce
selected names that not only enhanced the reading of his plots, but reflected on Irish culture, as well; surnames like *Ryan, O'Brien, O'Connor,
Fitzgerald, Sullivan, Murphy, Hayes, O'Connell, Walsh,* and *O'Donnell*—
names that have remained among the most common in Ireland since
the 1659 census (MacLysaght 29)—deliberately people the pages of
Joyce's canon. Of course, the names *Dedalus, Earwicker,* and *Plurabelle*
are glaring exceptions: Stephen is asked a number of times in *A Portrait*
and *Ulysses* what kind of name he has, and both Buck Mulligan and
John Eglinton refer to Stephen's name as "absurd" and "fantastical";
HCE's and ALP's names are also the subject of conjecture in *Finnegans
Wake*, especially when the washerwomen gossip about the couple in
chapter 8. The provenance of these particular names, however, will be

dealt with in later chapters, especially since they represent a deliberate departure from Joyce's usual practice of nominal verisimilitude.

In addition to contributing to the accuracy of Joyce's Dublin manifestoes, actual names often provided Joyce with found humor, found irony, or found satire, and these he appropriated in various contexts throughout his writings. When a real name was rich with punning possibilities, Joyce used the name mercilessly. The Childs fratricide case of 1899, for example, a case Joyce drew upon for material in *Ulysses*, may have been attractive to Joyce because of the name of Samuel Childs's defense attorney, *Seymour Bushe*, mentioned by name nine times in *Ulysses* (6.470, 7.741, 7.742, 7.743, 7.748, 7.749, 14.959, 15.1000–1001, and 17.792). Fascinated with the trial itself, Joyce attended the proceedings and took notes. Though he may have been drawn to the Childs murder case for a number of reasons, among these his interest in familial unrest and the battle for filial omnipotence which he inscribes in Nausicaa and in *Finnegans Wake*, Joyce also may have found the case interesting because of the onomastic possibilities and the comic pluralities of the *Bushe* name. Eric Partridge, in his *Dictionary of Slang and Unconventional English,* identifies *bush* as a mid-nineteenth and a twentieth century slang term for pubic hair, citing the turn-of-the-century mock proverb "A push in the bush is worth two in the hand" (161–62); and Joyce uses *bush* in this sense in the last sentence of Lotus Eaters when Bloom envisions himself reclined in the bath, "the dark tangled curls of his bush floating" (*U* 5.570).[5] Although the name *Seymour Bushe* sounds like a bad dirty joke, and although it is a name one might accuse a writer of making up, it is characteristic of the kind of name that attracted Joyce the onomastician, and for that reason, because it contains a serendipitous pun, Joyce immortalizes Seymour Bushe, and names like *Seymour Bushe*, in his writings. He also capitalizes on the name of Bushe's defendant, and the phrase *Childs murder* modulates in the Oxen of the Sun episode into a phrase signifying the murder of children, erupting into issues of infanticide, abortion, and contraception (*U* 14.958, 14.1017). Joyce exploits the semantic and paronomastic possibilities of real names, especially those drawn from contemporary culture.

Joyce was one of those writers on whom nothing was lost. As A. Walton Litz said of Joyce's art, "No piece of information was too irrelevant to find its place in the comprehensive pattern" (5) of what Joyce referred to as "mosaics" (*Letters* 1:172). Joyce had a wealth of literary and historical documents from which to collect his material, as well as a number of makeshift clipping services at his disposal in the form of relatives and friends around the world. Their cooperation, coupled with his own extensive and monumentalized research, allowed Joyce to file reference on top of reference, ever ready for recall. Joyce's great intellectual archive teemed with collected trivia, according to Frank Budgen, mundanities that would find their hour upon the loom of days:

> [Joyce] was a great believer in his luck. What he needed would come to him. That which he collected would prove useful in its time and place. . . . I have seen him collect in the space of a few hours the oddest assortment of material: a parody on the *House That Jack Built*, the name and action of a poison, the method of caning boys on training ships, the wobbly cessation of a tired, unfinished sentence, the nervous trick of a convive turning his glass in inward-turning circles, a Swiss music-hall joke turning on a pun in Swiss dialect, a description of the Fitzsimmons shift. (175)

Given this information, it is not difficult to imagine Joyce collecting, as he did other things, names, particularly names that would heighten the comic, the ironic, the grotesque in his texts. In his study of the composition stages of *Ulysses* Michael Groden reveals how Joyce's revision process often incorporated the inclusion and revision specifically of names and lists of names—deleting names, changing spellings of names, and including others. He quotes Joyce's letter to his printer in November 1921: "If you have not already passed pp. 294 & 295 will you please insert in the list of names *after* 'Goosepond Prhtr Kratinabritchisitch' *and before* 'Herr Hurhausdirektorpresident etc. the name; 'Borus Hupinkoff' " (165). Joyce spent many hours revising and evaluating *Ulysses*—as this letter surely indicates—but it is important to note that he also paid particular attention to names in his texts, and that catalogues of names, individual names, and associations of names were also singled out in the revision process. Gifford explains that while the *Hupinkoff* inclusion contains an obvious pun on the name *Boris Godunov*, "an additional aspect of the pun [is that] in May 1907 Joseph Conrad's son Borys had a severe and disturbing attack of whooping cough" (*"Ulysses" Annotated* 335).

We might imagine Joyce's pleasure at the *Hupinkoff* discovery, since he most likely enjoyed the onomastic pun on whooping cough. Joyce often entertained himself by "translating" names, using translation to extract further comic or ironic significance from names. In a 1906 letter to Stanislaus, Joyce writes of some recent translations:

> A clerk here is named (he is round, bald, fat, voiceless) Bartoluzzi. You pronounce by inflating both cheeks and prolonging the u. Every time I pass him I repeat his name to myself and translate 'Good day, little bits of Barto'. Another is named Simonetti: They are all little bits of something or other, I think. (*Letters* 2:202)

Joyce also translated his own name, telling friends that *Joyce* meant the same thing in English as *Freud* meant in German. Some of Joyce's most intriguing nominal translations, however, occur in *Ulysses* when Stephen pairs off the names of *Cicero* and *Podmore*, *Napoleon* and *Goodbody*, *Jesus* and *Doyle*: "—Sounds are impostures, Stephen said after a pause of some little time, like names. Cicero, Podmore. Napoleon, Mr Goodbody. Jesus, Mr Doyle. Shakespeares were as common as Murphies. What's in a name?" (*U* 16.362–64). His list is an elaborate word puzzle that centers on name translations, as Robert Adams explains in *Surface and Symbol* (223). *Cicero* is from the Latin *cicera* ("chickpea"—the name first given to one of the orator's wart-ridden ancestors). *Chickpea* is something akin to *Podmore* in English; the *Napoleon* reference is supposed to suggest to the reader the emperor's last name, *Buonoparte*, hence the *Goodbody* Joyce couples the nominal reference with. *Jesus*, anointed, oiled, suggests to the mind of Stephen the name *Doyle*. It is interesting that Stephen's list of names is hierarchical, pitting famous men with exotic names—*Cicero*, *Napoleon*, and *Jesus*—against men whose names are representative of a lower class, names that have high incidence in Ireland. *Doyle* and *Murphy*, for example, are among the more common surnames in Ireland. In *Irish Families*, MacLysaght identifies *Doyle* as the twelfth most common surname in Ireland, and ranks *Murphy* as the most common—a fact, no doubt, corroborated in episode 16 of *Ulysses* when Murphy reveals his surname and earlier in Joyce's work when the unnamed protagonist in "An Encounter" suggests that his friend answer to the alias *Murphy* (*D* 26), choosing for himself the name *Smith* because of its high incidence not only in America (a fact probably garnered from his compulsive reading about the Wild West [*D* 19–20]) but in England and Ireland as well.[6] The young boy may also have chosen the name *Smith* for himself because it suggests a kind of artisan, as in *goldsmith* or *silversmith*, and is therefore a figure for the artist. Moreover, *Smith* strengthens the early narrator's association with the artisan Daedalus and suggests that the young boy who is central to the first three stories in *Dubliners* is a precursor to Joyce's later Daedaelean figure.

For all its commonness, *Murphy*, the name assigned to Mahony in "An Encounter," remains a name representative of the Irish working class, and this is why the Citizen clamors over its representative dismissal from the list of births and deaths in the *Irish Independent*. As David Seed explains, "The Citizen's point is of course that even these names symptomize the extent of English colonial rule over Ireland, but Joyce ridicules his narrow nationalism by preceding this episode with a ludicrous name-list and by giving the spurious sailor in Eumaeus the very name which the Citizen presents as all-Irish, namely Murphy" (48).

When Stephen uses *Murphy*, however, saying that "Shakespeares were as common as Murphies," he seems to be forwarding the argument that naming is destiny; his deliberate pairing of the exotic with the mundane seems to argue just that. His list is noticeably international in scope, incorporating the Latin *Cicero*, the Corsican *Napoleon*, the Aramaic *Jesus*, and the Norman English *Shakespeare*, and pairing each of these with a typical and nondescript Irish name. The name *Doyle*, for example, is a depressing foil when placed next to the name *Jesus*, just as the name *Podmore* pales in comparison beside the name of the thundering orator *Cicero*.

Doyle, especially when paired here with *Jesus*, is an interesting name not only for its use in *Ulysses* but for its frequent use in *Finnegans Wake*, particularly in the trial scene of 3.4 (*FW* 573–76) where *Judge Doyle* (574.09), *Judge Jeremy Doyler* (575.32), and a jury "of stout fellows all of whom were curiously named after doyles" (574.31–32) figure in adjudicating the Umbrella Case. Most likely, here *Doyle* puns on the *Irish Parliament, An Dail;* but it is also telling that Joyce assigned the name *Doyle* to his "After the Race" character Jimmy Doyle, the man who represents the Irish "race" in that story. Often taken as a commentary, one of a number of Joyce's allegories of Irish historical relations, "After the Race" details the hoodwinking of a young, naive, socially uxorious twenty-six-year-old, one in the story's international quartet of "hilarious youth" (*D* 44), in an all night card-playing session. The internationally distinct names of some of the other characters in the story—

Ségouin, Rivière, Villona—suggest the relations between Ireland and its European allies. Pairing *Doyle* with *Jesus* as Stephen does in his Eumaeus word puzzle, he seems to be arguing that naming has little to do with destiny. An exotic name, a socially prominent name, a genealogical hapax legomenon—these guarantee nothing. Stephen skillfully balances his argument by coupling the names of successful achievers with names that are common and indigenous in Ireland.

If we recall Stephen's prejudicial assessment of common names in *A Portrait*, when he says contemptuously of the name *Dolan*, "Dolan: it was like the name of a woman that washed clothes," and argues to himself about Fr. Moran that his "name and voice . . . offended his baffled pride: a priested peasant, with a brother a policeman in Dublin and a brother a potboy in Moycullen" (*P* 55, 221), we see that Stephen's callousness about low names has softened.

When we meet Stephen in *Ulysses* he argues that names have nothing to do with success, adding that even the name *Shakespeare* was as common as the name *Murphy*, an indication that the next great national poet could be an Irishman whose name was one of high incidence in Ireland. Joyce ideally blends the two nationalities in *Ulysses* when he lists among the heroes and heroines of antiquity "Patrick W. Shakespeare" (*U* 12.190–91), cleverly merging his own nameling, Patrick W. Joyce, with the name of the Elizabethan bard, once again suggesting the Irishness of the next Shakespeare, and forcing us to use the name *Shakespeare* as Joyce uses it, as a common noun denoting "poet." Joyce clearly derived the same pleasure from the name of a Clontarf publican, Patrick Byron, whom he mentions in *A Portrait* (164). Stephen's proclamation that "Shakespeares were as common as Murphies" suggests as well that Shakespeares were a dime a dozen, as common as potatoes, since *murphy* means potato in the Irish vernacular. The term even makes it into Shem the Penman's "new Irish stew" (*FW* 190.04), a recipe for *Finnegans Wake* itself that incorporates a melange of ingredients. While Stephen muses on naming and destiny in *Ulysses*, we begin to understand Joyce's own preoccupation with the complex matrix of names, the suggestibility of names, how they might shape or control one's destiny. And while Stephen indicates his own reluctance to accept the sociological consequences of a name, he is the victim of such a name himself, and he alludes to that irony a number of times in *A Portrait* and *Ulysses*.

Joyce's own preoccupation with names and naming manifests itself in his texts; Joyce invests his characters with names that smack of the real, the comic, the magical, or the ironic in an attempt to achieve verisimilitude—to represent not only "real life" but his own life, since Joyce's characters mimic his own behavior and follow his own curiosities and interests, translating names, as he himself does, and investing their own literary creations with names of real people. Stephen's reference in the Parable of the Plums to Kate Collins, for example, identifies her as proprietress of the North City Dining Rooms (*U* 7.940), a position that a woman by that name actually held in 1904 (Benstocks *Who's He* 69). Since Joyce created his works in a genuine spirit of autobiography, he was careful to cull from his own biography real or representative names of friends, enemies, and acquaintances to inhabit his fiction, thus adding at the very least to the nominal and biographical veracity of his literary texts and at the very most to his patient and detailed self-portrait. Like the topographical identification of Finn's body in the early pages of *Finnegans Wake*, Joyce's image, too, is embroidered into the pages of his works, and often it is his rhetoric of nomenclature that reveals him.

Although Joyce's Shem is said to have "scrabbled and scratched and scriobbled and skrevened nameless shamelessness about everybody ever he met" (*FW* 182.13–14), Joyce often maintains a partiality and a fidelity to names, leaving only an important few shamelessly unnamed. While literary namelessness used to be a fate designed to marginalize characters in fiction, a reflection of their unimportance, a marker (ironic in its absence) that distinguishes them from the primary cast of characters, modernist writers challenge that notion, and many of them leave nameless the very protagonists of their texts. A number of modernists, male writers in particular, leave their protagonists unnamed: Samuel Beckett's hero in *The Unnamable* is nameless, and his *Not I* presents characters known only as Mouth and Auditor; Pirandello's *Six Characters in Search of an Author* contains six nameless main characters; Auden's "Unknown Citizen" is a tribute to someone known only as JS/07/M/378; the protagonist of Ralph Ellison's *Invisible Man* is unnamed; Flann O'Brien's novelist in *At Swim-Two-Birds* is nameless; and Franz Kafka's K. in *The Castle* as well as his Joseph K. in *The Trial* remain, to a degree, nameless. Namelessness, it seems, has become for male modern writers a *riposte* with which to reply to the whole question of identity. In modern literature, though, nameless characters are no longer mute, no longer entirely powerless, and certainly, no longer marginal.

Joyce's works contain a wealth of nameless figures, characters who, regardless of their importance, are afforded no names in the text. Shari and Bernard Benstock enumerate the many anonymities in *Dubliners* in their *Who's He When He's at Home*, where they cite the onomastic anomalies of important characters in "The Sisters," "An Encounter," "Araby," "Eveline," "Two Gallants," "Counterparts," and "Clay" (4). They also refer to Joyce's "tight economy in awarding names to his characters" (3), noting that Joyce attached his own given name, *James*, to three characters in *Dubliners*, and that he assigned, in particular, the names *Tom*, *Jack*, and *Joe* to not a few of his characters (3–4). Given Joyce's preoccupation with names, it is tempting to speculate on why so many Toms, Jacks, and Joes people his texts. Why is Joyce so frugal with names, and is it only to mirror "the narrowness of perspectives and possibilities in Dublin," as the Benstocks suggest (4)?

The use of common names that are bland enough to avoid particularization is known as "slotting" names. The use of names such as *Tom*, *Jack*, and *Joe*—names that have wide popular appeal—allows the least amount of intrusive connotation on plot and imagery. Charactonyms, so often a staple of literary interpretation, meddle with plot and action, which may explain not only Joyce's tight economy in naming his *Dubliners* characters but also his repeated use of the popular given names *James*, *Tom*, *Jack*, and *Joe*.

In his discussion of Christian names in *Irish Families*, MacLysaght gives statistics of incidence for the names *John (Jack)*, *Thomas*, *James*, and *Joseph*. Although he uses as his sources only the counties Limerick, Clare, Donegal, and Offaly, we can still get a sense of the popularity of the names during the first half of the twentieth century: for every hundred males in each of the four counties, approximately eighteen were named John [Jack], nine were named James, seven were named Thomas, and four were named Joseph (39). These names, then, account for 38 percent in a representative sampling of males.

While verisimilitude in naming is an important element of Joyce's allusive method, another element of Joyce's naming process is his use of names as literary and cultural echoes. The names of Masters Goff and Shapland Tandy, for example, which occur in Stephen's Goulding vignette in the Proteus episode of *Ulysses* (*U* 3.81), are aurally reminiscent of Laurence Sterne's *Tristram Shandy*—that is, the name *Shapland Tandy* sounds like a spoonerism of Sterne's title. While the antiquated language of the Goulding vignette contributes to its suggestiveness— the words *coign of vantage, nuncle, hillock, moiety,* and *morrow* are etymonic throwbacks to linguistic days of yore—aural references like *Shapland Tandy* compose only part of Joyce's allusive method, as Joyce often used sounds and words that smacked of something else, incorporating into his works items that by design were redolent and allusive— whether the implied comparison came from a homophonic, alliterative, syntactic, or rhythmic source.

But the allusion to *Tristram Shandy* is a false one—it only reeks of literary import: James Goff and Shapland Morrie Tandy were actual tax officials in 1904 Dublin; Joyce gleaned their names from *Thom's* (98, 2022). Often selecting names that carry literary or cultural echoes, names that give the reader a false lead, names that, in their very precocity, tease the reader into misappropriating an otherwise good hunch, Joyce manipulates the reader unwittingly to participate in the name game. Names are rarely to be trusted in Joyce—and in *Ulysses,* Madden can attest to that, having lost a handsome bet on Sceptre "for a whim of the rider's name" (*U* 14.1126): the rider, a jockey named *Madden.* Just when a name seems propitious, just when a name would seem to be working *for* a character, Joyce creates an opposite effect, mocking, at various points in his texts, the magic of onomancy, while using it to his advantage at other places in his texts—as in the case of the *Dedalus* name, since the legacy of Stephen's name is almost half the story of *A Portrait* and *Ulysses.*

Joyce warns us against trusting names in Eumaeus where Stephen discusses the fraudulence of sounds, noting that their deceit lies in their ability to trigger associations. "Sounds are impostures . . . like names" (*U* 16.362–63), Stephen decrees in an episode that questions the very constructs of naming. First, Bloom suspects that *Murphy* is not the sailor's real name—this reminds us of the "Let you be Murphy" alias uttered by the unnamed narrator of "An Encounter." Second, Bloom notes the improbability of the correspondence between the name on the postcard produced by the sailor (*A. Boudin*) and the sailor himself. Third, the name *Dedalus* gets tossed around mercilessly in the episode when Murphy confuses Simon Dedalus with a performer he saw in Stockholm in Hengler's Royal Circus. Moreover, the identities of the food served in the cabman's shelter are questioned:

although it is called coffee, the narrative voice questions its resemblance to the real thing, referring to it as a "cup of what was temporarily supposed to be called coffee" (16.360) and an "untastable apology for a cup of coffee" (16.1141). In an amusing commentary on the chapter, Robert Bell points out that "the awful coffee in the cabman's shelter, for example, may be called 'whatever you like to call it,' but it remains defiantly static, petrified, solidified; beneath the Penman's whimsical variations, we recognize the 'whatever you call it,' and wish the narrator would wake up and smell it" (193–94). The bread suffers the same fate, being called a "socalled roll" (*U* 16.366). What we have in Eumaeus is a series of nominal challenges, since names, descriptors, and identities are suspect throughout the entire episode. New epithets are constantly being applied to characters in the cabman's shelter, for example. Murphy becomes "the communicative tarpaulin" (16.479), "the Skibbereen father" (16.666), "the impervious navigator" (16.1010–1011), "Shipahoy" (16.901), and "Jack Tar" (16.1456), almost as if he were given a newer, more animated, moniker with every mention. Moreover, Joyce's curious use of pronouns in this chapter—"he purposed (Bloom did)"; "He, B, enjoyed the distinction of"; "he (B.) couldn't help feeling"; "Alluding to the encounter he said, laughingly, Stephen, that is"; and "It will (the air) do you good" (16.1866–1867, 16.1495, 16.1049, 16.231–32, 16.1718)—makes it seem as if, in a chapter so concerned with impostures, Joyce is showing how language conceals as much as it reveals, how language always relies upon or requires a sort of parenthetical aside for true clarity. Ordinarily transparent pronouns are deliberately rendered opaque and in need of interpretation in this chapter of *Ulysses*.

As soon as Bloom acknowledges the "curious coincidence" of the Simon Dedalus namelings (16.414), the sailor offers up yet another nominal coincidence. He identifies himself as Murphy, "D. B. Murphy of Carrigaloe" (16.415), using a surname that Stephen and Bloom had been discussing moments earlier, and one whose initials, *D. B.*, might represent the names *Dedalus* (D) and *Bloom* (B). While Murphy's surname corroborates Stephen's recent proclamation that "Shakespeares were as common as Murphies," the sailor may have adopted the name *Murphy* as an alias because he overheard their recent discussion of the name. Murphy is carrying papers that identify him as the discharged D. B. Murphy he claims to be (16.452), but his pockets seem to be filled with paraphernalia that might identify him in other aliases, *A. Boudin,* for instance, the name on the messageless postcard he produces.[7] More important, Bloom tries to get Stephen to give Murphy not his real name but an alias. Aware of the capacity for deceit that is implicit in names and sounds, Stephen resists Bloom's urging and gives his real name instead, ignoring the "warm pressure" from Bloom's kicking boot:

> The redbearded sailor who had his weather eye on the newcomers boarded Stephen, whom he had singled out for attention in particular, squarely by asking:
> —And what might your name be?
> Just in the nick of time Mr Bloom touched his companion's boot but Stephen, apparently disregarding the warm pressure from an unexpected quarter, answered:
> —Dedalus. (16.367–74)

Murphy phrases his question as if to invite a pseudonym, and it is interesting that Bloom, by kicking Stephen, tries to get him to forward an alias, as well, particularly since Bloom's nominal history is not pedigree, his father having changed his name by deedpoll from *Virag* to *Bloom*, and his maternal grandfather having changed his name from *Karoly* to *Higgins*. In *Joyce and the Jews*, Ira Nadel explains the likely politics behind the name change:

> In 'Eumaeus' Bloom admits to Stephen that *his* name has been changed (16.365–6); Virag, of course, became Bloom, an act coinciding with Leopold's birth. Bloom marks the importance of this shift by keeping the newspaper announcement of his father's legal change of name in the second drawer of his dresser (17.1869–72). Characterising this Jewish adjustment to the Irish world, there was also a name change on Bloom's mother's side; her father, Julius Higgins, was born Karoly, a Hungarian name that itself was most likely changed from a Jewish one, or, more precisely, purchased since at that time Jews were forced to give up their names and pay for new ones. (144)

That Bloom's maternal grandfather most likely inherited a purchased name only to change it himself is important, since this sort of nominal trafficking is indeed simonious, reminding us of the young narrator's obsession with the words *gnomon, simony,* and *paralysis* in the opening pages of *Dubliners*. We have seen how Joyce exploits the *gnomon/nomen* connection. Perhaps the simony reference hints at nominal commodities, too, since a number of names in *Dubliners, A Portrait, Ulysses,* and *Finnegans Wake* are bought and sold.

   While legal name changes constitute an important element of Joyce's naming process, a number of characters skirt the legal route, selecting, instead, aliases and adopting false names: *Murphy* and *Smith* of "An Encounter," Little Chandler's dreamy pen name *T. Malone Chandler,* Gabriel Conroy's "*G. C.,*" Simon Dedalus's multiple name changes to evade bill collectors as well as those used to pawn family belongings, *Virag's* name change by deedpoll to *Bloom,* a noticeably Anglicized spelling of the overtly Jewish name *Blum,* Bloom's maternal grandfather's name change from *Karoly* to *Higgins,* Bloom's own *Henry Flower* pseudonym, and lord Harry's intricate name change detailed in Oxen (*U* 14.625–32), to name but a few. Joyce also adds to his list of characters the names of real people who adopted aliases—*Junius,* for example, a name appended to Bloom in the Cyclops episode, was the pseudonym of the unknown author of letters that appeared in London's *Public Advertiser* from 1769 to 1772. *James Lovebirch,* too, is probably a pen name, as it is redolent of the names usually adopted by writers of pornographic novels. In fact, Mrs. Yelverton Barry accuses Bloom in Circe of making "improper overtures" (15.1021) to her under the pen name of James Lovebirch (15.1016–1024). Similarly, *Leo Taxil* is the pen name of *Gabriel S. Jogand-Pages,* and *Simon Lazarus* the presumed real name of Shakespeare's biographer *Sidney Lee.* Further, in Joyce's circle, *Ettore Schmitz* took the pseudonym *Italo Svevo, Paul Leon* was born under the patronymic of *Leopoldovich,* and Joyce himself often wrote under the pen name of *Daedalus,* signing reviews, articles, and letters to friends with that name, as well as a number of other interesting and playful names, such as *Mr and Mrs Ditto MacAnaspey, MacGinty,* and *W. B. Yeats*—signatures that will be discussed in detail in a later chapter.

   Moreover, both Stephen and Bloom create aliases for themselves, second selves, others, to whom they address their own criminal accusations. Remembering his short stay in Paris, Stephen recalls a characteristic defense:

> Yes, used to carry punched tickets to prove an alibi if they arrested you for murder somewhere. Justice. On the night of the seventeenth of February 1904 the prisoner was seen by two witnesses. Other fellow did it: other me. Hat, tie, overcoat, nose. *Lui, c'est moi.* You seem to have enjoyed yourself. (3.179–83).

Stephen's defense, "*Lui, c'est moi*" (I am he), is all the more curious when it is resounded by Bloom upon his being accused by The Mob of being "as bad as Parnell," a veritable "Mr Fox":

BLOOM

(*excitedly*) This is midsummer madness, some ghastly joke again. By
heaven, I am guiltless as the unsunned snow! It was my brother Henry.
He is my double. He lives in number 2 Dolphin's Barn. Slander, the viper,
has wrongfully accused me. (15.1767–1771)

What is ironic about Bloom's incensed reply is that he defends himself
against charges that would align him with *Mr. Fox,* Parnell's well-
known alias, by enlisting as his defense his own alias, *Henry Flower.*
Moreover, Bloom's reply, rich with Shakespearean allusion, is in fact a
hodgepodge of plagiarized verses from *Twelfth Night* and *Cymbeline.*
Thus, he defends himself against Lenehan's cry "Plagiarist! Down with
Bloom!" (15.1734) with the very evidence needed to condemn him, erasing with his alibi the protective nature of his alias. Just a few pages
earlier in that episode, Bloom answers Ben Dollard's query, "Pansies?"
by suggesting that they "Embellish (beautify) suburban gardens"
(15.1665–1667). Again, Bloom's very defense incriminates him, since
his use of *beautify,* the word that vilified Shakespeare in Greene's *Groatsworth of Witte,* seems to substantiate Lenehan's imminent accusation,
just as Stephen's defense—"Other fellow did it: other me. . . . *Lui, c'est
moi*"—incriminates him. Both men shield themselves from blame
while admitting to their own participation in the alleged crime by blaming their self-generated doubles.

   Though his defense undoes him, Bloom's pseudonym *Henry Flower*
is an important name to examine. While appropriate as a pseudonym
for Bloom, the name is doubly propitious not only because his ancestral surname *Virag* means *flower* in Hungarian, hence, the *Bloom* into
which Rudolf changed it, but because Bloom often associates his penis
with the word *flower,* referring to it in Lotus Eaters as "the limp father
of thousands, a languid floating flower" (5.570–71). The Bloom/
Flower/penis connection yields further irony when Cissy Caffrey refers to Bloom in Nausicaa as "*uncle Peter*" (13.535), a name he solicits
not only because he is standing by a rock, but because he is standing
by a rock playing with his "peter," a slang term for the penis as early as
the nineteenth century. The name is even translated into French in
Circe when it appears as *Henri Fleury* in connection with the sexual
violation of Mrs. Dandrade (15.3003), and it is translated into Portuguese as *Senhor Enrique Flor* when it is listed among the forest wedding
participants in Cyclops—*Senhor Flor* characteristically presiding "at

the organ" (12.1288). The name also metamorphoses into *Don Poldo de la Flora* (18.1428) once Molly gets hold of it in Penelope. But Bloom's epistolary pseudonym *Henry Flower* is interesting for a number of other reasons, as well, and a close reading of the name yields important information about the character, just as it offers readers essential information about Joyce's nominal scheme.

First, *Henry* is a German name, a name that traditionally means ruler of the house. Bloom's choice of this pseudonym may indicate his wish to be the firmly established ruler of the Bloom house, if he is not already. Second, Bloom uses the flower as a metaphor for his genitals, but the flower is usually a metaphor for the female pudendum, according to the *Oxford English Dictionary* and various dictionaries of slang. Bloom's reference to his penis as a flower, "a languid floating flower," hints at his androgyny, especially since many flowers contain both male and female sexual reproductive parts. Bloom is indeed a "womanly man," as he is referred to in Circe (15.1799), an accusation anticipated in an earlier pun in the Oxen episode—"womanly bloom" (14.676). The name *Henry Flower* allows Bloom the fantasy of being the dominating, sexual, virile ruler of the house while at the same time it admits to the unlikelihood of such. Bloom's choice of the name *Flower*, then, is an interesting one, since it is a name that carries with it the sexual connotations so often associated with him. *Flower* is a name that typifies Bloom's character. It is a name that is appropriate, but it is also a name that demands to be considered specifically because it is self-generated.[8]

To be sure, all names in literature, as well as those in life, demand to be considered, and one does not have to be an onomastic zealot to find names, their meanings, and their provenances attractive, as a fascination with names is not confined to popular culture. Leonard Ashley, in an essay that expounds the rhetoric of literary onomastics, explains why names need to be addressed, and how an examination of names can reflect or expand an author's intentions:

> We study how names, as well as how other words, are suited to the structure in which they are arranged, first to the purpose, second to the nature and capacity of the likely audience. We see how names help create the characters in a work of fiction and connect them with the literary strategy, the readership and its experience, the cultural context, and the rest of the real frame of reference. . . . We also see how names

expose the author's investment of self in the work. ("Mudpies which
Endure" 11–12)

We often try to gauge a relationship between a person and his or her
name, attempting to establish a connection between names and people, names and things; and although some names remain unintelligible, "innocent," perhaps, of any subtext or underlying meaning, the
many decipherable names lend meaning to Joyce's artistic and allusive
methods, and can assist our interpretation. Often, the literary onomastician is seen as one who operates not on an objective but on a
subjective level, gathering information about names in a text through
instinct and personal observation—what the names suggest to her or
to him. But often these very principles govern the invention of names
for literary characters. Ashley recounts that "when an admirer told
Thomas Mann that the character name *Chauchat* was only one letter
away from the French word for 'hot cat,' the very deliberate writer
replied, 'I never thought of that, unless unconsciously' " (*What's in a
Name?* 205). While Ashley admits that Mann "may have been speaking
with tongue in cheek," he argues that instinctive, subconscious, or unconscious factors figure as prominently as an author's conscious delib-
erations when placing names on anything (205), and it is precisely our
assumptions about the names writers use that lead to discovery.

Literary naming, in itself, allows for certain assumptions on our
part, inviting, and then preying upon, our expectations. In one of the
earliest tracts on naming, Plato's *Cratylus*, two friends of Socrates argue
about the appropriateness of names. Cratylus insists that *Hermogenes*
cannot possibly be his companion's name, and argues that there has to
be a natural appropriateness between the name of something and the
thing itself. There needs to be a link—a semantic agreement—between
a person and his name, Cratylus argues, but Joyce characteristically
takes advantage of such a philosophy, one that would demand a logic
between the name and the named.

In *Finnegans Wake* he mocks such an attitude. Before listing eighteen
names for HCE, whose initials spell HERE COMES EVERYBODY
(88.21–23), Joyce argues that HCE's multiple names "fit" him, and that
he *looks* like his names: nicknamed Here Comes Everybody by the populace (32.18–19), "an imposing everybody he always indeed looked"
(32.19), we are told in an onomastic aside, an afterthought that reinforces the idea that naming is logical, while it tests at the same time

the boundaries of naming and expectation; that is, HCE's nickname seems inevitable and justified, since he "always indeed looked" like everybody anyway. While Joyce was not the first to parade the absurdity of onomastic magic, or the first simultaneously to support it, his works feed upon our notion that naming reveals identity, a concept he might have noted from Lewis Carroll's *Alice's Adventures in Wonderland* and *Through the Looking-Glass,* although Joyce claimed in 1927 not to have read either.

Carroll's *Alice* books continually challenge relationships between names, naming, identity, and destiny. In the trial scene in chapter 11 of *Alice's Adventures in Wonderland,* for example, twelve jurors are busy scribbling notes before the trial even begins; so Alice ventures to ask what they are writing:

> "What are they doing?" Alice whispered to the Gryphon. "They can't have anything to put down yet, before the trial's begun."
> "They're putting down their names," the Gryphon whispered in reply, "for fear they should forget them before the end of the trial." (115)

Of course, in Joyce's handling of a similar trial scene in *Finnegans Wake* (3.4), the jurors are assured of the ability to remember their names since, like the judge, each is named *Doyle.* Part of Carroll's onomastic genius, however, lay in his ability to create comic effects through incongruous naming, as he does when his Alice, surrounded by characters with names like *White Rabbit, Mad Hatter, March Hare,* and *Cheshire Cat,* meets up with a lizard named *Bill.* Naming, in other words, becomes increasingly disjunctive; that is, instead of providing expected linguistic clues, names rupture logic, especially in nonsense literature, a tradition from which Joyce drew heavily. What Carroll is playing with in passages such as these is a fact that he and Joyce, no doubt, appreciated: that names *needn't* be reflective of the objects they name. Carroll's nonsense literature always presumes, if not demands, an incongruous correspondence between name and identity, since therein lies the humor and nonsense. In the "Looking-Glass Insects" chapter of *Through the Looking-Glass,* for example, Carroll parodies philosophic theories that identify relationships between names and identity. In "Looking-Glass Insects," the names of the insects predetermine what they look like, and while these are not names per se, but names redefined as common nouns, one can still find traces of Carroll's onomastic philosophy within the examples. The Rocking Horsefly appears in Tenniel's drawing as just that, for example—a rockinghorse fly. In addition, the names of the insects that appear in that chapter supersede the names of the insects that Alice identifies: the bread-and-butter-fly supplants the butterfly, for example, and the snap-dragon-fly displaces the dragon-fly. Naming as a whole in the works of Carroll is a process, a day to day modulation based on reason, no matter how ridiculous. Humpty Dumpty's name, for example, means the shape he is, he tells Alice (209). In this respect alone, Carroll seems to have influenced Joyce's onomastic maneuvering in that even the multiple names for his characters are nonsensical but fortuitous at the same time; and even the numerous renderings and reincarnations of names contribute to character definition.

Given Joyce's admiration of Lewis Carroll, it is all the more curious that he would assign the name *Alice* to Bloom's penis in the Circe episode, assigning, as well, the names *Martha* and *Mary* to his testicles:

> BELLO
>
> [to Bloom] You will be laced with cruel force into vicelike corsets of soft dove coutille with whalebone busk to the diamondtrimmed pelvis, the absolute outside edge . . . creations of lovely lingerie for Alice and nice scent for Alice. Alice will feel the pullpull. Martha and Mary will be a little chilly at first in such delicate thighcasing. (*U* 15.2975–2982)

Joyce's name for Bloom's penis, *Alice*, is an example of his extended use of nominal puns, since Bloom's penis, like his Carrollian namesake Alice, must go into the hole. Such extended nominal play is evident in the names of Bloom's testicles, as well: named *Martha* and *Mary*, the names of Lazarus's two sisters, the names remind us that Bloom's penis, like Lazarus, is the object of resurrection. The nameplay here may be more serious, however. The names *Martha* and *Mary* might cause readers to recall Martha Clifford and Molly Bloom, since *Molly*, like *Mary*, is a diminutive of *Marion*. If *Martha* and *Mary* refer to Bloom's two adult lovers, then perhaps the *Alice* reference is meant to suggest Milly Bloom, the young object of Bloom's sexual musings, as well, according to those who subscribe to the incest theme in *Ulysses*. If this reading of the Alice, Martha, Mary trio is accurate, then Bloom's genitals encode the names of his three seductresses in this Circean enactment of Bloom's sexuality.

What is so amusing about Carroll's nameplay is that his character names often interrupt logic instead of corroborating it—and for many of us, naming should seem logical and not gratuitous. That is, if someone's name is *Richard Best*, for example, such as the character in Stephen's library audience in Scylla and Charybdis, we expect him to be "best," we expect him to bear the name as if it were a sort of destiny, as if it were an induction, as if it were an endowment, something Stephen mocks when he thinks of Richard Best as the best of three brothers: "Good. Better. Best." The exaggerated end of this belief is caricatured when Joyce uses names as rebuses or visual puns—something I will discuss below—but the link between names and identity has always been believed to be a magical one, an ominous one, and James Frazer identifies its existence in even the most primitive of cultures in *The Golden Bough.*

Yet this primitive, totemic belief is widely subscribed to today. Novelist Ralph Waldo Ellison, for example, considers his name to have been endowed with magical qualities, as is evidenced from this excerpt from an autobiographical sketch:

> In the dim beginning, before I ever thought consciously of writing, there was my own name, and there was, doubtless, a certain magic in it . . . neither could I understand what a poet was, nor why, exactly, my father had chosen to name me after one . . . he named me after someone called Ralph Waldo Emerson. . . . Much later, after I began to write and work with words, I came to suspect that he was aware of the suggestive powers of names and of the magic involved in naming. (Seeman "Unconscious Meaning" 239)

As Ellison suggests, naming carries with it a good deal of superstition, and in addition to the magical link that one expects to exist between naming and character, we assume, as well, that names are somehow deserved, and whenever possible, we feel comfortable appending such deserving names onto people in the form of nicknames and tagnames—and this is another element of Joyce's naming process. The name of the *Portrait* character *Tusker Boyle*, for example, is appropriate, since Boyle's fascination with his fingernails, his "tusks," as it were, is compatible with the cognomen *Tusker* (*P* 42–45). Further, his second nickname, *Lady Boyle*, is also appropriate, since his effeminate behavior specifically invites the name. Although the two nicknames coexist, they contradict each other, since *Tusker* is rich with phallic suggestion while the name *Lady Boyle* suggests Boyle's feminization. Although Ste-

phen remembers that Boyle got the name *Tusker* because "he had said
that an elephant had two tuskers instead of two tusks" (*P* 42), the name
probably stems, as well, from Boyle's adolescent buggery. In fact, another Clongowes student, *Athy*, one who makes riddles that turn on his
own name ("a thigh"), alleges that Boyle and Simon Moonan had been
caught smugging with some fellows in the square (*P* 42). Indeed,
Boyle's names are ascribed to him because of his behavior; that is, the
names are not behavioral determinants, as Ralph Ellison argues of his
own name, but behavioral consequences. Here, they corroborate logic
instead of interrupting it.

But names often function in a literary text as determinants, predict-
ing, instead of reflecting, the physical character and personality of a
character. When names begin to function as such, they undermine the
text, they compromise the very concept of characterization, affording
the writer a form of semantic shorthand, an economical form of characterization, and taking on even greater significance as the characters
become more spirited, more animated, and more distinctive.

Finnegans Wake, for example, permits the brief appearance of an
obese, disguised ex-nun named *Carpulenta Gygasta* (99.09). The name
itself serves to caricature and stereotype the character, since it not only
bespeaks but corroborates her corpulence, giganticism, and sluggish-
ness across at least three languages: L. *corpulenta* (corpulent), Gr. *gigas*
(giant), Sp. *lenta* (sluggish). Where once characters themselves were
sources of amusement, names in the *Wake* take on comical aspects of
their own, reducing the complexity of a number of characters; and
when naming itself becomes a vehicle for satire, the human complexity
of a character is reduced to a one- or two-word descriptor, "turning the
character into a mechanical doll, as Bergson observes, and heightening
the external ugliness (or *turpiditas*) of the charcter that Cicero claims is
the source of laughter" (Burelbach "Names" 171). Names in the *Wake*
often seem more comical than anything else, as if they populate the
text for no other reason than to heighten the comic absurdity; but that
is a dangerous assumption. Most of the names can be explicated using
sources like Adaline Glasheen's *Census,* or Roland McHugh's *Annotations,* since the names are comical renderings, hilarious twistings of
names of preexisting characters in literature, mythology, history, and
the *Wake* itself: Osti-Fosti (48.31), Sordid Sam (49.21), fireworker oh
flaherty (80.8–9), Posidonius O'Fluctuary (80.28–29), Morbus O' Somebody (88.14), Rhian O'kehley (90.28–29), Oirisher Rose (92.18), Pun-

chus and Pylax (92.36), Mayhappy Mayhapnot (110.07), Hanno O'Non-hanno (123.32), Toffey Tough (249.29), Sir Somebody Something (293.n2), Abdul Abulbul Amir or Ivan Slavansky Slavar (355.10–11), and Owllaugh MacAuscullpth the Thord (532.8–9), to name but a few. Joyce's fooling with the patronymical designation *O'* and his appending gratuitous *O*'s to characters' names constitute a sizeable portion of his nominal foolery in the *Wake*, and it is something he practiced with comical success in *Ulysses* where he added the prefix *O'* to the names of *Bloom, Bergan, Dignam,* and *Nolan,* creating, of course, *O'Bloom, O'Bergan, O'Dignam,* and *O'Nolan,* affording the characters an amusing mock chieftain status (*U* 12.216, 12.290, 12.374, 12.1183). Satire, then, shifts Joyce's aesthetic of burlesque to a different playing field—that of onomastic caricature. The name becomes comical because of its deterministic powers, because it lives up to and fulfills our glib, superstitious expectations. In the *Wake*, names read somewhat more like Old English kennings than names, since they are often two or more nouns linked together to convey an immediate visual image, as in the example studied above, *Carpulenta Gygasta*. The name, then, moves from being a source of identification to being something else: the name is a word picture—a rebus—and a comical or ironic one, at that. Not quite allegorical, the names are visual; the names are totemic, as in the name *Cockshott* (524.14), and often contain Joyce's commentary, as in the name *Ratatuohy* (342.24), one of Mr. Whaytehayte's "three buy geldings," no doubt a cynical rendering of *Tuohy* that is comical, visual, and culinary.

Rebuses abound in Joyce. Stephen's boyhood antagonist *Heron,* for example, looks like a bird: "[Stephen] had often thought it strange that Vincent Heron had a bird's face as well as a bird's name" (*P* 76). Reinforcing the link between name and identity, and strengthening the comedic obsurdity of the name *Heron*—the boy has a "high throaty voice"—he even uses language that is appropriate to his nominal circumstance, saying to Stephen in *A Portrait*, "I was just telling my friend Wallis what a *lark* it would be . . . " (75 emphasis added). Like the primitive totem, Heron's name, his clan, his tribe, as it were, is manifested in a visual image on his face. The features that distinguish him are the "flushed and mobile face, beaked like a bird's," the "shock of pale hair . . . like a ruffled crest," and the "thin hooked nose . . . between the closeset prominent eyes which were light and inexpressive" (76). Heron wears the badge, the mark, of his name.

As Michael Ragussis explains in his *Acts of Naming: The Family Plot in Fiction*, one's name is often "branded into the flesh as a sign of the outcast's shame" (39), citing as literary examples Dickens's Oliver Twist and Hawthorne's Pearl Prynne, characters whose lineage is literally "imprinted" upon them. Ragussis adds that "fiction suggests that the body actually bears the name as the ultimate mark of identification" (40), discussing Lewis Carroll's Humpty Dumpty in those terms:

> The most blatant version of this idea occurs in *Through the Looking-Glass*, with Humpty Dumpty looking "as if his name were written all over his face." The name written on the face, of course, represents what Humpty Dumpty argues (via Cratylus) in his philosophic debate with Alice: a name expresses the essential being of the thing named. . . . the child [is] marked from the beginning; in such a plot, to trace the child's genealogy is to read it in the marks that make his face an unofficial but entirely natural document. In seventeenth- and early eighteenth-century language philosophy, the terms *mark* and *name* are used almost interchangeably, and in the tradition I am describing, the marked face tells one's name. (40)

The name, then, becomes totemic—something both visual and stigmatic. Heron's surname functions as a pun, and when the name is a visual pun, when a name begins to function as such, characterization as we know it takes on a new slant.

Exactly how does naming function in the *Wake*, where Joyce's policies of naming become exhaustive? Characters are named and renamed forty and fifty times over in the *Wake*, and while this is nothing new— Leopold Bloom is given over seventy names in *Ulysses*—Joyce displays a rampant provection of naming in *Finnegans Wake*, where one name invites and generates another. In *Finnegans Wake*, names are almost always in flux, changing their form or spelling frequently throughout the dream, suggesting, in part, the fluid nature of *Wake*-an identity. How, though, can we take naming seriously when it seemingly becomes inconsequential, or when it is no longer limited by traditional literary onomastics?

When Stephen Dedalus echoes Shakespeare's nominal query, asking in Scylla and Charybdis, "What's in a name? That is what we ask ourselves in childhood when we write the name that we are told is ours" (*U* 9.927–28), his question is more than a literary allusion to his

Elizabethan predecessor; it is an utterance that signals his realization not only of the importance of names—personal names, cognomens, agnomens, surnames, patronymics, and matronymics—but of their function in the literary text. He later echoes the same line in Eumaeus, and Bloom responds, "Yes, to be sure. . . . Of course. Our name was changed too, he added, pushing the socalled roll across" (16.365–66). Here, the emphasis is not only on the arbitrary and artificial nature of family names but on the illogical and sometimes faulty bond between names and things, since the phrase "socalled roll" communicates the very questionable relationship between the two.

Heron's name is not so odd when placed on the continuum of onomastic history, since the origin of family names was not arbitrary; in fact, the earliest Irish surnames stemmed from physical, and as Joyce explains in the *Wake*, occupational agnomens (Adams 81; *FW* 30.15); but the "logical" connections between person and name began to fade sometime around the fourth or fifth century when patronymical systems of identification were introduced in Ireland, and a system of hereditary surnames was put into general use (Briffault 94; MacLysaght 45). Although many Irish popularly maintain that High King of Ireland Brian Boru "invented" the tradition of hereditary surnames, sides are divided on this issue: some argue that Boru only enforced and made compulsory the patronymical system that was in use but minimally during his reign. Boru, in fact, used no surname himself; it was appended, however, and in regular use some forty years after his death by his descendants who named themselves after him, placing the designation *O'* before Boru's personal name, and naming themselves after him as *O'Briain* (anglicized as O'Brien). Boru is credited with having introduced patronymics, i.e., *Mac*, meaning son of, and *O'*, meaning descendant of; but regardless of who "invented" the surname, most genealogists agree that Ireland was one of the first countries to adopt a system of hereditary surnames (a system that was introduced as early as the fourth century). Joyce's use of rebus word puzzles in his character names and tag names seems to signal a return to early naming correspondences; that is, names like *Heron* and *Cranly* and *M'Intosh* and *Mackerel* suggest the physical characteristics of their counterparts—a naming practice Michael J. O'Shea refers to as "physiognomic metonymy." Once the name becomes a rebus, a visual rendering, it begins to function as an allusion, as an implied reference.

Just as each name embodies an attempt at "defining" a character, each sustains an authorial attempt at corroborating physical or behavioral anomalies and distinctions.

An allusive name often supports understandings conveyed through other means in the text, as in the cases of Molly's name *Gea-Tellus*, Bloom's name *Elijah*, and Stephen's name *Wandering Aengus*; but it also functions in Joyce's works to undermine the text by misleading and misdirecting the reader—especially when the name is rich with allusive significance. *Beatrice*, for example, a name assigned to one of the women characters in Joyce's *Exiles*, is a name that recalls the youthful object of Dante's affection while at the same time it transfers the qualities of Dante's Beatrice onto Joyce's—qualities of youth, innocence, beauty, virginity, and goodliness—thereby misrepresenting and ironizing Joyce's character so that her name works to remind us of what Love once conventionally was and of what it has become.

Although Dante's Beatrice was to conduct the poet from a terrestrial to a celestial paradise, Joyce's Beatrice holds no such office; instead, she inspires Richard Rowan to glorify the earthly, and it is the temporal and not the celestial that is the subject of his art:

RICHARD

If I were a painter and told you I had a book of sketches of you you would not think it so strange, would you?

BEATRICE

It is not quite the same case, is it?

RICHARD

[*Smiles slightly*] Not quite. I told you also that I would not show you what I had written unless you asked to see it. Well? . . . Would you like to see it?

BEATRICE

Very much.

RICHARD

Because it is about yourself?

BEATRICE

Yes.

(*Exiles* 16–17)

While Beatrice's role as Muse links her with the Dantean figure, her last name, *Justice*, also aligns her with her Italian nameling since the Italian

Beatrice's father, Folco Portinari, not only was one of the fourteen Buonomini instituted in 1281, but also served several terms as Prior—one of the ruling magistrates of the republic of Florence—from 1282 to 1287 (Toynbee 436). In addition, Beatrice's brother is alluded to by Dante in *La Vita Nuova* as his next best friend after Guido Cavalcanti, and there are a number of interesting parallels among the Dante, Cavalcanti, and Portinari triad, and it is specifically Joyce's use of names that hints at the allusive correspondences.

Significantly, Guido Cavalcanti married a Beatrice, daughter of the famous Farinata, in 1267; in addition, while Dante served as Prior during the summer of 1300, he was haplessly instrumental in sending his friend not only into exile but to his death as well, since Cavalcanti died two months later as a result of the effects of the malarious climate into which he had been banished (Toynbee 130). Friendship betrayals, amorous love, Dante, Beatrice, heaven, hell, infernos, and the dispensation of justice are all connected to each other and echo vociferously within the framework of the name *Beatrice Justice*. In the case of the name *Beatrice* alone, then, we can see how Joyce's allusive method works and how it is ushered and introduced weblike from his philosophy of naming. Allusive names ask to be deciphered, and like Joyce himself, the reader needs to elaborate upon their thematic potential.

When Joyce uses an allusive name, the textual consequences can vary in a number of ways. First, the reader can be misled by assuming a correspondence between the character and his or her name and personality. This has led to a variety of approaches to Eveline, the heroine of the story in *Dubliners,* whose only crime is her characteristic misfortune of having the name *Eve* embedded in her own. An allusive name such as *Eveline* can expand an individual character's fate to supra-individual dimensions. For example, Eveline's rejection of Frank is ironic—not pathetic, not predictable, and not unanimated; rather, it is forceful, meaningful, and jarring specifically because she is nominally tied to Eve, who is known for her inability to resist temptation. In refusing to go with Frank, Eveline acts unpredictably; her resistance—while many classify it as expected, given her situation, her passivity, her promise to her mother, her Catholicism, which she invokes at the pier—is anything but expected. She does not live up to her name, and, as a consequence, she triumphs. Her allusive name not only lends that degree of victory to her situation, but it paints the circumstances with irony. Seeing Eveline as actively resistant (rather than passively terrified) depends on seeing her also in charge of her emotional life, and though all the seas of the world are tumbling about her heart as she clutches at the railing like a frenzied animal, Eveline breasts the current and takes charge in the moment that concludes the story, her allusive name notwithstanding.

T. S. Eliot was the first to inquire about Joyce's allusive method when, in "Ulysses, Order and Myth," he gave it a name, proclaiming that Joyce's "mythical method" made the world suitable for art. Thinking, no doubt, of his own "mythical method," Eliot praised Joyce's use of the Homeric parallels, but not everyone agreed with the inventiveness of Joyce's Homeric superstructure. Ezra Pound's comment on the Homeric framework of *Ulysses* is important to our understanding of Joyce's allusive method because Pound's judgment is an early assessment and it yields an understanding diametrically opposed and complementary to Eliot's. Both Pound and Eliot defend, early in the critical tradition, the extremity of Joyce's allusions and, by extension, their own. Pound explains:

> These correspondences are part of Joyce's medievalism and are chiefly his own affair, a scaffold, a means of construction, justified by the result, and justifiable by it only. The result is a triumph in form, in balance, a main schema, with continuous interweaving and arabesque. (406)

Pound's judgment raises an interesting question, namely, when are a writer's correpondences or literary parallels justified? When is an allusion justifiable? Joyce was so indiscriminate in his use of allusion, so uninhibited by his audience's lack of knowledge, that much of his writing remains unintelligible, resisting our many attempts at exegesis. Because Joyce incorporated into his texts allusions no matter how small, no matter how impenetrable to his audience, countless allusions remain, to a degree, Joyce's "own affair," as Pound called them. But not all allusions are difficult, and even the obscure ones function in much the same capacity as the transparent ones: allusions often function as associations, intimating complex patterns of associations that bind Joyce's works together. Joyce uses allusions to order his and his characters' impressions and memories, and to comment on their experiences. His allusions in the epic mode point out, often ironically, the magnitude of everyday life. Moreover, they act as networks of correspondences and function to corroborate character traits, to maintain the humor of a text, and to forge personality.

Although T. S. Eliot argued in "Tradition and the Individual Talent" that "not only the best, but the most individual parts of [a writer's work] may be those in which the dead poets, his ancestors, assert themselves most vigorously" (48), the chorus of ancestors who vigorously "assert themselves" throughout the Joyce canon is not always mellifluous. Often, they rage against Joyce's encapsulating forms and his experimental language. Shakespeare, for example, who looms so heavily in Joyce's *Ulysses*, can be traced in Joyce's use of nomenclature throughout his oeuvre where the range of Juliet's oft-repeated "What's in a name?" is given full romp, fair play, and fastidious nominal attention. From *Stephen Hero* through the *Wake*, Joyce's use of names is tied to his philosophy of naming, and it affects the narrative of his texts. Through naming, Joyce comments on religious distinctions (Protestant, Catholic, Jewish), on British and Irish history, on sexuality, on comedy, on patriarchy, and on the literary forms of satire and irony. More than sources of amusement, more than indications of ancestry, and more than identifying geneaological tags, names in Joyce are windows into his artistic method: they reveal the artist's maneuvering hand, his intention, his framework, his literary superstructure.

While it is important to follow Joyce's naming processes from *Stephen Hero* through the *Wake*, it is perhaps most interesting to start by following the *patterns* he created, to see how Joyce's nominal tomfoolery grew from the initial stages of onomastic experimentation, and to see how Joyce fashioned his knowledge of names and naming out of an aesthetic cemented in linguistic and semantic panache. By the time Joyce arrived at *Finnegans Wake*, he had already done some recycling— not merely a recycling of names, but a recycling of the associations of names, a recycling of the allusive, comedic suggestions of names.

The name *Bags Comisky*, for example, which occurs in the Eumaeus episode of *Ulysses* (16.205–6), prefigures Molly's commentary on the male body when she thinks in Penelope, "compared with what a man looks like with his two bags full and his other thing hanging down out of him or sticking up at you like a hatrack no wonder they hide it with a cabbageleaf" (18.542–44). Corley suggests that Bags Comisky is someone "Stephen knew well out of Fullam's" (16.206), though Stephen does not seem to recognize the name; but the name *Bags Comisky* might remind a reader unwittingly of the nearly debagged Clive Kempthorpe discussed in the beginning pages of the novel (1.160–71), since Bags's surname may come from the Latin *commiserari: Com*, with; *miserari*, to pity; *miser*, wretched, pitiable. Another name that comes full circle is one of Bloom's self-penned anagrams, *Bollopedoom* (17.408). The imperfect anagram Bloom made of his name in childhood comes back to haunt him in the name *L. Boom*, the name printed in the newspaper account of Dignam's funeral, since both *L. Boom* and *Bollopedoom* are missing an *l.*; not coincidentally, *Old Ollebo, M. P.* (17.409), another of Bloom's anagrams, is also missing a letter—this one, an *o*. By making two of Bloom's four anagrams imperfect, Joyce adds to the comedy of his character by having Bloom bungle the spelling of his own name not once, not twice, but three times, since Bloom's answer "L." in response to Hynes's query "What's your Christian name?" seems to be responsible for the orthographic error in the newspaper. Again, Joyce seems to be corroborating our sense of Bloom's lack of talent at writing and wordplay, since Bloom cannot work out a simple anagram. The name *Cockburn* (12.231), one of the names listed in the obituaries of the *Irish Independent*, is reminiscent of the names *Paul de Kock* and *Poldy Kock*, and anticipates "*Messrs Achburn, Soulpetre and Ashreborn*" in *Finnegans Wake* (59.17–18), whose names suggest not only the ache and burn that Joe had associated with Cockburn in *Ulysses* when he grimaced, "I know that fellow . . . from bitter experience" (12.233), but the impotence-inducing saltpeter ("Soulpetre"), the slang *peter*, and the phoenixlike resurrection of the aching and burning phallus in an eternal erection ("Ash-reborn"). A similar name in *Finnegans Wake*, *J. P. Cockshott* (524.14, 524.16, 524.34), also resounds with a host of phallic associations because the reader has grown used to Joyce's naming techniques and patterns; and like Stephen and Madden, two of Joyce's characters who bemoan the infidelity of names, we, too, find it increasingly difficult to take names at face value because we have been taught, since *Dubliners*, how to regard names and how to read them.

Names also echo cross-referentially within and between texts, often creating balances and counterbalances. Ironically, because no names are given to the protagonist of the early *Dubliners* stories, a continuity is established within and between the first three stories. In *A Portrait*, comparably, Dante Riordan's name is nicely balanced by the mention of other Dantes, Edmund Dantes of Dumas's *Count of Monte Cristo* (*P* 62–63) and Dante Alighieri (*P* 252); similarly, the "deephen" and "Reephen" of *Stephen Hero* (*SH* 165) prepare the way for the "Steeee-eeeeeeeephen!" emitted by Stephen's trailing ashplant in *Ulysses* (*U* 1.629); furthermore, we might recall Farrington's miscopied *Bernard*

Bodley (*D* 90), his "twice Bernard," as it were (Bernard Bernard), when we see Madame Blavatsky nee Hahn-Hahn written as "twice Mrs Hahn" in *Finnegans Wake* (*FW* 66.23). In addition, *Bos Bovum*, the good bog Latin name given to Lord Harry's bull in Oxen of the Sun (*U* 14.628–29) is recalled in *Finnegans Wake* in the phrase "a bull, a bosbully" (*FW* 490.34–35). *Pimply Meissel* of *Giacomo Joyce* (*GJ* 6) prefigures Joyce's later physiognomic metonymy *Nosey Flynn,* and both metonymic names resound with Stephen's pronouncement against the Christian Brothers in *A Portrait:* "their piety would be like their names, like their faces" (*P* 166). This characteristic mannerism, where names echo one another across Joyce's texts, makes it seem as if Joyce picks up on or perpetuates in later works a nominal joke he missed out on earlier, or one he did not exploit enough, letting the proverbial shoe drop years later (as in the name *Shouldrup* [*FW* 157.10]), delivering in retrospect a punch line or an onomastic jab to jar the memory.

The connection between names and faces was given amusing treatment at the Venice Symposium in 1988. Toward the close of his paper, "The Visual Pun in *Finnegans Wake,*" Michael J. O'Shea repeated a joke about an armless and nameless Quasimodo-like figure who was hired by a local church to work in the bell tower. Lacking arms, the unnamed Quasimodo would ring the bells with his face, and when he fell from the tower to his death one afternoon, none of the horrified onlookers could identify him to the police. One man came close, however, admitting to the crowd that although he could not recall the man's name, his face, he said, rang a bell. An assortment of names in Joyce's works "ring bells"; that is, they are descriptive; they function to establish the connections between faces and names. Even the "Nameless One" of *Ulysses* is appropriately named in this context, since he appears later in Circe with a "featureless face" (15.1143). The implication here is that if one has no physical characteristics to detail in onomastics, no name to match the face, no tag to highlight that which separates him from others, then one is doomed not only to physiognomic anonymity but to onomastic anonymity as well, since names are so often linked in Joyce to physical and personality distinctions.

Clearly, names resonate in many different and complex ways in Joyce's texts. The discernable patterns, the recycled jokes, the careful attention to names in the texts—all these indicate Joyce's wide-ranging and canny interest in the meaning and complex functions of names. It is obvious that Joyce began to recycle and reuse patterns that he had established with success throughout his works because he knew that names, like sounds, trigger associations, and he found in naming one more method of layering and texturing his prose. The repetition of naming patterns and techniques adds to the richness of Joyce's works and to their complex texture of allusions, intensifying each nominal reference, and firmly establishing yet another element of his allusive method; that is, Joyce alludes to patterns he, himself, set in motion, not only using onomastics to comment on contemporary culture, history, and literature, but using the rhetoric of nomenclature, his nominal tomfoolery, to comment on his own works.

CHAPTER TWO

Naming and History

It is easily conceivable that Joyce thought of himself as Clio with a sense of humor—as a Muse of history, not only empowered to create or inspire history but also licensed to refashion it comically. In such an office, Joyce could meddle with history, shaping it to fit any comical, aesthetic, ironic, or exaggerated mold, not only making an improved history but merging the genres of literature and history in a way that had been censured by nineteenth-century writers like Macaulay. Macaulay chided early historians such as Thucydides, who often fabricated historical speeches and invented dialogue, arguing that their practice "violates, not only the accuracy of history, but the decencies of fiction" (154). As his historian forbears had done, Joyce guiltlessly blurs the boundaries between fiction and reality, stretching history until it functions for him as a system of poetics (Orr 2). In *Finnegans Wake,* for example, "history" becomes "his story"—a form of written narrative that is as susceptible to distortion as any other form, often distinguished by falsified, misleading, misinterpreted, embellished, or fictionalized facts. In the *Wake* Joyce frequently exploits the thin line between history and fiction, as he does in "Storiella as she is syung" (267.07), a phrase that fuses the word "story" with the Italian words for "history" (*storia*) and "lie" (*storiella*). It is Joyce's creative use of history—his comedy and his license—that I will examine in this chapter, particularly as it affects his rhetoric of names and naming.

In the Irish scheme of things, literature and history are not just parallel, they are nearly identical. James Matthews explains that "for an Irishman, a situation or event is an opportunity to amplify the minute into the monumental, to invest the trivial, isolated reality with mythic significance" (73). From this tradition, then, emerges Joyce, whose literary and stylized embellishments of moments past and present warrant exploration. Clearly, for Joyce, every moment has historical potential if it is handled by the right storyteller.

History, for the Moderns, was something dubious and irresolute; it was the nightmare, Stephen would argue in the Nestor episode of *Ulysses*, from which he was trying to awake (2.377). Complicating and intensifying the horrors of the Great War were recent revolutions in physics that redefined one's relationship to the universe, specifically, Einstein's Theory of Relativity, the Second Law of Thermodynamics, and the Quantum Theory. To be sure, the Quantum Theory was the most historically disturbing of the three because of its unvarnished message of cosmic uncertainty, as Alan Friedman explains:

> In a word, the current interpretation of quantum theory is that the theory requires *uncertainty*. An observer of atomic particles disturbs the particles he or she is measuring in an irreducible manner. The more carefully you measure the position of an electron, the more you might be disturbing its motion, so that any knowledge of its motion becomes less precise. That is one direct outcome of the "Heisenberg Uncertainty Principle." (200)

It was the Uncertainty Principle, Friedman argues, that shook the Modern literary imagination most violently, causing people to question the very structures of truth and knowledge, and to impugn the foundations and motivations of history itself. Formulated in 1927, the Uncertainty Principle seemed to confirm the imprecision of science and history, assuring Moderns not only that any pursuit of knowledge would cause commotion, upsetting a silent harmony, however slight; but that scientific inquiry could never attain accuracy since it is a pursuit grounded in imperceptible disturbance, and a man-made fiction, however pragmatically successful, rather than an inevitable way of seeing the world.

Joyce codifies his response to the troubling Uncertainty Principle not only in the way he uses words and names but in the way he views history, as if it were a continuous negotiation in the aftermath of what physicists half-jokingly refer to as the Butterfly Effect: "the notion that a butterfly stirring the air today in Peking can transform storm systems next month in New York" (Gleick 8). Names, particularly those in *Ulysses* and *Finnegans Wake*, need to be read in terms of the Butterfly Effect, as if the history of a character's names, her or his placement on a personal continuum of names, has brought the character to the point at which we see her or him for the first time. Any other way of reading names in Joyce would sacrifice complexity for rigor, counting the stripes on a tulip.

Joseph Millin suggests that Joyce was prescient not only of the Uncertainty Principle but of late twentieth-century theories of chaos, as well:

> Though Joyce could not have known much, if anything, about Chaos Theory, the study that strives to understand the relationship between randomness and order, deterministic predictability and uncertainty, the study that attempts to explain how order emerges *from* randomness, how randomness acts as an inexhaustible source of creativity, and how randomness is its own unique form of order, Joyce's works respond in unique ways to recent changes in quantum physics, extending language and language theory beyond the uncertainty principle. (12)

More so than his Modern contemporaries, Joyce discovered that language, too, was a matrix of complex dynamics, and that the written word exposes inconsistencies and defies any attempt at precision. Capitalizing on what he saw as the "brain's immense capacity for ambiguity and random association" (Millin 1), Joyce formulated a matrix of chaos, taking advantage of, exploiting even, our blessed rage for order.

It is precisely this "rage for order" that compounds the reader's anguish when approaching names and naming in Joyce, since names behave like intervening variables, "toppling the order that the reader strives to establish, introducing new variables into play, perpetuating the dialectic and urging the reader toward ever more complex associations, creating multiform combinations, changing the rules as the game is played, forging new forms of order out of the eternally creative wellsprings of chaos" (Millin 16). The metamorphoses of names, their constant states of flux, their teasing randomness, and their historical significance—these will be examined in this chapter.

Joyce would have appreciated Karl Marx's statement about history if he had heard it, that "history repeats itself; the first time as tragedy, the second as farce" (Hassan 106), since Joyce's use of history is often a dramatic blending of the two. Considering the fame of Marx's quotation, and the number of books with Marxist orientation in Joyce's Trieste library, it seems plausible that Joyce would have known the quotation, especially since the phrase, in one way of thinking, describes Joyce's *Ulysses* in a nutshell. From Joyce's early critical writings—indeed, from his earliest, "Et tu, Healy"—Joyce's use and misuse of history are characteristic of his writings. Joyce saw himself as the eternal author, historiographer, cartographer, cosmographer, and hagiographer for his race—and his fascination with history was unvarying. Joyce had a well-noted enthusiasm for military history, scientific history, literary history, philosophic history, and, of particular interest here, onomastic history—and his love of history fueled his study of the history of names.

Joyce was probably a regular reader of the weekly *Irish Times* column "Irish Family Names," for example, since Dominic Manganiello has identified that column as a source for the inaccuracy of the Finnegans' coat of arms in *Finnegans Wake* (Manganiello 30–31). A pious reader of "Irish Family Names," Joyce would have been familiar with the genealogy of an assortment of Irish surnames, not least among these his own, as is often indicated in his writings where he plays with the origins and genealogies of surnames to form an historical, a comic, or an ironic pattern. One example of this occurs in the Oxen of the Sun episode of *Ulysses* where Joyce inscribes his dual enthusiasm for names and history by charting among the episode's other charted progressions the history of Irish nomenclature, as we shall see. Oxen is a large portion to chew—but even in small, digestible bites, we can see how Joyce manipulates names throughout his works to comment on, fictionalize, and reinvent history.

One of the most amusing historical names to conjure with in *Ulysses* is the name of the Dublin eccentric nicknamed *Endymion*, whose full name was *James Boyle Tisdell Burke Stewart Fitzsimons Farrell*. Joyce alters the name in *Ulysses* to exploit its historical suggestiveness, as we shall see, and to avoid libel, referring to him as *Cashel Boyle O'Connor Fitzmaurice Tisdall Farrell* (10.1102). Joyce's rendering of Endymion's string of names is interesting for several reasons—not least among these the fact that he excises his own given name *James* from the list, replacing it with *Cashel*, a name suggestive of the prominent Irish ruin. From Endymion's string of names Joyce also eliminates *Burke* and *Stewart*, names reminiscent of Thomas Henry Burke, murdered in Phoenix Park by the Invincibles in 1882, and Charles Stewart Parnell, accused in 1887, via forged letters, of having approved of the murder. The names carry not only political import but religious significance as well, since both Burke and Parnell were Protestants. By removing *Burke* and *Stewart*, Joyce avoids sacriliging Parnell, and "Catholicizes" Endymion. Joyce replaces both their names with *O'Connor*, suggesting Daniel O'Connor, the Liberator, and Rory O'Connor, the last high king of Ire-

land. Joyce also changes the name *Fitzsimons* to *Fitzmaurice*, erasing the
reference in *Fitzsimons* to Stephen Dedalus's father, Simon, and replacing it with a reference to Stephen's younger brother, Maurice, shifting
nominal focus from Dedalus *père* to Dedalus *frère*. The prefix *Fitz*, however, from the French *fils*, signifies "descendant of" in an Anglo-
Norman genealogy. Moreover, the *Oxford English Dictionary* notes that
the designation *Fitz* often indicated an illegitimate offspring (266).
Given these overtones, then, it seems that Joyce deliberately eliminates
any reference that might be read as *descendant of*, or *son of*, Simon, by
purging the suggestion of Dedalian paternity from Farrell's name,
disempowering Simon as father throughout the book, that is, and clear-
ing any indictment of Simon as consubstantial father—something Stephen will try to disprove to his library audience in Scylla and
Charybdis.

Apart from his fascinating string of multiple names, Endymion was
an interesting character in his own right, a walking spectacle, as Richard Ellmann describes him:

> There was 'Endymion' Farrell, who carried two swords, a fishing rod,
> and an umbrella, who wore a red rose in his buttonhole, and had upon
> his head a small bowler hat with large holes for ventilation; from a
> brewer's family in Dundalk, he was said to have fallen into a vat and
> never recovered. (365)

Farrell was a popular Dublin eccentric; indeed, he is even listed and
discussed in the turn-of-the-century Dublin publication *Dublin Eccen-
trics*. Though Joyce wrestled with and manipulated Farrell's names in
1922, Oliver Gogarty tried to make sense of them as well, fifteen years
later, in *As I Was Going down Sackville Street*, where he includes an ink
sketch of Endymion in the early pages of the book. Because Gogarty
lends particular attention to Endymion's string of names in *As I Was
Going down Sackville Street*, his novel is important to our understanding
of Joyce's naming process and its relationship to history.

When he discovers Endymion's name in the National Library signature book, something that Stephen imagines doing in chapter 9 of *Ulysses* with much the same result (9.1115–1116), Gogarty offers an on-the-
spot analysis of Endymion's multiple names, saying,

> "Damn his symbolism . . . he's got my name and the names of my
> friends and acquaintances included in his title. There's George's, Joe's

and the Shamuses'. You've escaped [he says to Father McQuisten].
What's the idea?"

"Whist!" said Father McQuisten.

"He cannot have been christened in all the surnames he has included
in that line—that almost reads like one of Phoebus Apollo's gaseous
hexameters!"

"No one can say for certain why he has made a conglomeration of the
present-day well-known citizens, and taken their names to himself unless . . . he may mean that he represents in his person an amalgam of the
ingredient races that go to make up the nation."

"He means that he is Ireland? Poor devil!"

"Its countless Jameses, the Norman, Elizabethan, Cromwellian con-
querors, merchants and mediocrities—all the incomers, in short, that
make up the Irish mosaic."

"That he is a walking amalgam?"

"Or that the Irish Farrell has to bear on his back all the rest of them—
Normans, Elizabethans, etc. Or that he is leading them in triumph—
settlers, planters, merchants and mediocrities, as well as the Shamuses
of the people. So he is a nation in himself." (9)

It is interesting to see how Gogarty's Father McQuisten dismantles
Endymion's name, linking its genealogy with a pattern of Irish colonial
history; but it is even more interesting to see how Joyce refashioned
Farrell's historical name in 1922, supplanting one version of Irish history with another.

Farrell's multiple surnames are engaging specifically because they
suggest a political and ironic Irish history; and the nickname *Endymion*
is interesting, as well, since its allusiveness confirms our sense of the
character's lunacy. Gogarty's keen examination of Farrell's names, however, helps to identify an understated irony behind the character's brief
appearances in *Ulysses*, particularly in the Wandering Rocks episode
where Joyce details the British viceregal procession. Clive Hart and Leo
Knuth have already detailed the topographical wanderings in the episode, showing how the diverse patterns of procession intimate the
form of a Union Jack, an ironic emblem to present itself on a Dublin
intersection but one nonetheless befitting a viceregal cavalcade. In fact,
Joyce inscribes in Wandering Rocks a purposeful "mistaking" of the
Grand Canal bridge for the Royal Canal bridge when he mockingly
refers to the *Grand Canal* bridge as the *Royal Canal* bridge only because
the viceregal is passing over it: "At the Royal Canal bridge, from his
hoarding, Mr Eugene Stratton, his blub lips agrin, bade all comers wel-

come to Pembroke township" (*U* 10.1272–1274). Such an error of voli-
tion befits the occasion of a visiting Excellency.

Apart from that ironic renaming when Joyce fuses naming and history, the theme of British colonial rule is intensified further by Farrell's
presence in the episode, since, as Gogarty argues, "the Irish Farrell has
to bear on his back all the rest of them—Normans, Elizabethans, etc."
(9). Endymion is representative, then, not only of Irish genealogical
history, but of Irish political history; and it is his name—certainly nothing else—that indicates his political importance in the chapter. Farrell's
political significance may be one reason why he stares "through a fierce
eyeglass across the carriages at the head of Mr M. E. Solomons in the
window of the Austro-Hungarian viceconsulate" (*U* 10.1261–1263). Importantly, he grimaces not only at the British and Irish extravaganza but
at the enthusiastic Austro-Hungarian participation as well. Whether
one of Joyce's ways of commenting on the fruitless correspondence
that Arthur Griffith saw between Hungary and Ireland in *The Insurrec-
tion of Hungary,* or a textual reminder of Bloom's Austro-Hungarian
roots, Endymion's grimace in the direction of the Austro-Hungarian
viceconsulate compounds the political tension in the episode. While it
is obvious that genealogical history mirrors political history, the two
brands of history feed off each other, as we shall see.

Though Joyce's narrative manipulations of history have been well
documented,[1] his manipulations of onomastic history need critical illu-
mination not only because they remain a mystery to onomastic novices
but because they illuminate Joyce's aesthetic use of history. Often align-
ing himself with Viconian and other popularized theories of history,
Joyce crafted his art around historical patterns of his own making—
much as Yeats did in *The Tower* and *The Winding Stair*—and it is particularly his use of onomastics that helps to reveal his method. Although
every name is a narrative in itself—for every name there's a story—
together they form patterns, nominal designs, that constitute part of
Joyce's allusive method and illustrate or re-create patterns of history.

Another example of Joyce's creative use of onomastics and history is
discernable in a short passage from *Finnegans Wake* that precedes "The
Ballad of Persse O'Reilly." The passage is emblematic of Joyce's use of
the technique in his earlier works. It is a discussion of HCE's names:

> Some vote him Vike, some mote him Mike, some dub him Llyn and Phin
> while others hail him Lug Bug Dan Lop, Lex, Lax, Gunne or Guinn.
> Some apt him Arth, some bapt him Barth, Coll, Noll, Soll, Will, Weel,

Wall but I parse him Persse O'Reilly else he's called no name at all.
(44.10–14)

John Bishop suggests that this is a "chain of patently absurd names . . .
representative of the string of names that runs through the book as a
whole" (131), names that work associatively, he says, "like the
dreamwork's condensed and 'composite structures,' to reveal underlying states and conflicts that befall 'this most unmentionablest of men'
in his drift through the night" (132). It would be absurd to think of any
of these names as the "real name" of the *Wake*-an hero, for example; but
the pattern of names listed here is important because it methodically
articulates a pattern of history.

In the Benstocks' essay "The Joycean Method of Cataloguing," an
appendix to *Who's He When He's At Home*, the authors point out that
while

> comic juxtaposition [is] often the main reason for selection [in a cata-
> logue], logical analysis may well be frustrated by a factor of sheer
> whimsy, but even extravagant absurdity is not necessarily without de-
> sign, and few would suppose that Joyce's artistry would allow for totally
> random inclusion [in any given Joycean catalogue]. (217)

Because there is most often a method in Joyce's nominal madness, one
needs to discover and articulate that method at each new crossing,
since blanket explanations and interpretations rarely suit more than a
singular passage perfectly.

The "some mote him Mike" passage in *Finnegans Wake* can be dis-
sected as follows: first, the name *Vike* indicates the Viking/Scandina-
vian presence in Ireland, establishing, at once, a national ancestry for
HCE. The name *Vike* is neatly balanced through rhyme with the name
Mike—a reference, most likely, to the archangel Michael but also to
the derogatory and slang appellation "Mick" for an Irishman; thus,
cultural and political tensions are apparent already in the first two
names of the series. "Some dub him Llyn" is a reference to Dublin, a
reference further corraborated by the name *Phin*, after the legendary
Finn, and later in the list by the name *Wall*, a name that recalls the
Magazine Wall, which surrounds a small fortification in Phoenix Park,
located near the legendary resting grounds of Finn MacCool as it is
described early in the *Wake*. Further, the double ("dub") "l" ("Llyn") is
a Welsh onomastic characteristic, as in the name *Llewelyn*, which

might also be the name most directly suggested here, a further indication of HCE's Celtic genealogy.

Next in the series is a quartet of three-lettered names, *Lug Bug Dan Lop*, and one might to begin to suspect that the number of letters in the name is a prerequisite for its inclusion in the list. Adaline Glasheen explains that "lug is an ear" (*Third Census* 156), so the *Lug Bug* half of the *Lug Bug Dan Lop* name translates into Earwig/Earwicker/perce-oreille/Persse O'Reilly. *Lugh* also gives us the sun-king of the Tuatha De Danaan, one of the five original races to invade and inhabit prehistoric Ireland—a balance that parallels the earlier Finn reference. The second half of the equation is more taxing, although McHugh identifies *Dan* as Daniel O'Connell, the Liberator (44), a reference that prefigures the *Persse* (Pearse) that will come later in the list, since Pearse, too, is popularly hailed as another Liberator. *Dan* is also a reference to King Daniel, one of the many kings alluded to in this passage, as well as an accepted synonym for *Danish* (*American Heritage Dictionary* 334)—so the name *Dan* balances the earlier name *Vike*, since both point to HCE's alleged Scandinavian origins. *Lop*, to cut away or trim or prune—a term used often in gardening—reminds one of the iconographic image of the young HCE hoisting a flowerpot on a pike (*FW* 30–31). Jumbled, however, the letters of *Dan Lop* spell out *Poland*, yet another national insinuation to reckon with, and a country whose history of colonization and oppression mirrors Ireland. *Dan Lop* may also be a reference either to John Boyd *Dunlop*, Glasheen suggests, a nineteenth- and twentieth-century English inventor and manufacturer of tires and other rubber products (*Third Census* 81), or to Daniel *Dunlop*, president of the Dublin Theosophical Society when AE (George Russell) was vice president (*Third Census* 80). The multiple suggestiveness of the name is important in this passage, since Glasheen notes that both Daniel and John Boyd Dunlop double for each other most of the time in *Finnegans Wake* (*Third Census* 81).

Next in the series are the names *Lex, Lax, Gunne,* and *Guinn*. Vico notes in *The New Science* that "Among the Romans, 'names' meant originally and properly houses branching into many families," adding that "in Roman law *nomen* signifies right . . . [and] in Greek *nomos* signifies law" (140–41). Thus the inclusion of the Latin word of law (L. *lex*) in HCE's list of names is an extended pun on naming and law. Moreover, prior to its founding by the Vikings, Dublin was a gathering place for Celts because the Liffey was rich in salmon—thus, the reference to salmon (lax), coupled with the references to law (perhaps Brehon Law, thought so barbaric by Edmund Spenser) and Guinness (*Guinn*), may be read as further indications of HCE's Celticity. The name *Gunne* corroborates HCE's Irishness while verifying an earlier name on the list, *Mike*, if *Gunne* is taken as a reference to Michael Gunn, manager of Dublin's Gaiety Theatre. Though the names *Mike* and *Gunne* suggest theatricality on the part of HCE, they also strengthen the dreamer's association with Ireland.

The alphabet dictates the next three names: "Some apt him Arth, some bapt him Barth, Coll." Baptism, the sacrament at which one is given a name ("thuartpeatrick" [*FW* 3.22]) and "primesigned" (*FW* 24.28), figures into the naming process here, and, by Catholic association, Saint Bartholomew, as well, whose symbol is the knife, an allusion to the one with which he was flayed alive. HCE, then, is aligned through naming with the martyred "Barth," but perhaps with the martyred Saint Stephen as well, whose Joycean namesake Stephen Dedalus is nicknamed "Kinch, the knifeblade" in *Ulysses* (1.55), and is referred to by Mulligan as a "priestified Kinchite" (9.555), a portmanteau qualifier that joins the concepts of ordination and beatification. True to the succeeding letter of the alphabet, the next name in the series begins with a *C, Coll. Arth* may be a reference to Arthur Guinness, validating the *Guinn* listed just before it. Grammatically, however, the name *Arth* is a squinting modifier: it looks in two directions and feeds semantically off both sides of the sentence that contains it, since *Arth* is also a reference to Arthur Wellington, listed shortly thereafter in the series as *Weel* (an orthographical and phonetic stand-in for *Well*, a more obvious truncation of the names Wellesley and Wellington, as Joyce uses it in *FW* 448.07). Also a reference to the legendary King Arthur of Britain, the name *Arth* provides a third sovereign precursor to the name *Soll* (L. *sol*, "sun") which follows later in the series, most likely a reference to King Solomon, often heralded as the wisest and most magnificent of the kings of Israel, but also a reminder that Arthur, "the once and future king," falls only to rise again. (HCE is also called a sun king in the *Wake*—thus the *Soll* inclusion here aligns the dreamer with Arthur, Solomon, and Louis XIV, the famed "sun king.")[2] Because Solomon was most celebrated for his building of the famous temple that bears his name, the reference to him here may confirm HCE's earlier and continuing connections throughout the *Wake* with Ibsen's Masterbuilder, not to mention HCE's countless nominal associations with Freemasonry

(*Bygmester Finnegan* [FW 4.18], for example), as well as his established relation to hod-carrier Tim Finnegan.

Directional names seem to pervade next in the list—*Noll* and *Soll*, as in north and south, an intimation of the Irish Partition. *Noll* is reminiscent of Cromwell, however, an agent of that Partition, since Cromwell was nicknamed *Old Noll* (McHugh 44). *Noll* is also a name associated with Shakespeare, Glasheen reports, since he is said to have played the Old Knowell role in Jonson's *Everyman in his Humour* (*Third Census* 157). Notably, then, in the names *Noll* and *Soll* lie associations with Cromwell, Shakespeare, Jonson, and Solomon. *Will*, which follows *Soll*, corroborates the Shakespeare in *Noll*, as does the name *Shikespowre* (FW 47.21), listed among the lyrics of the ballad proper where the name *Lord Olofa Crumple* (FW 45.03) is also listed, a reference that supports HCE's earlier connection to Cromwell via the name *Noll*. But the name *Will* also suggests another king, the fifth so far in a list composed of Arthur, Daniel, Lugh, and Solomon—William the Conqueror, referred to earlier in *Finnegans Wake* as "William the Conk" (FW 31.14). *Weel*, the name listed next, is a reference to Wellington, and *Wall*, the penultimate name in the series, is probably a reference to the Magazine Wall, a topographical anomaly listed in the first stanza of the ballad, and one of the many recurring motifs throughout the *Wake*. Glasheen glosses *Wall* as a reference that often points to *Will* (Shakespeare) whenever it appears (*Third Census* 300). *Persse O'Reilly*, the last name in the series, the rebus, the visual pun on the young pike-wielding, earwig-catching Earwicker (FW 30–31), also refers to Patrick Pearse, educator and leader of the 1916 rebellion, as well as the less mythologized *O'Rahilly*, also of the Easter Rising (McHugh 44).

The multiple names afforded HCE even in this short passage serve two roles: each suggests the character or personality of HCE, his breeding, his origin, his "nobility" or his ancestry, while also reinforcing at least one other element in the series. As a catalogue, then, this short example of twenty-one names is surprisingly cross-referential and dense. Names always carry messages, but in *Ulysses* and *Finnegans Wake* in particular, the arrangement of names carries messages as well, corroborating, undermining, or deconstructing the very message a single name or group of names implies. In the brief, monosyllabic list of HCE's twenty-one names above, a racial pattern emerges: HCE is identified by Scandinavian names, by Irish names, and by Polish, Danish, British, and Aramaic names. Just as Gogarty argued of Endymion's name, so might we argue of HCE's: "He [not only] includes the life of Dublin at the moment in himself" (82), but he includes "all the incomers . . . that make up the Irish mosaic" (9). Indeed, HERE COMES EVERYBODY.

Though Joyce's catalogue of Irish history in "The Ballad of Persse O'Reilly" is interesting because of its complex patterns of suggestion and association, Joyce also inscribed the "Irish mosaic" much earlier when, in Oxen of the Sun, he reproduced onomastic history. Oxen of the Sun reportedly traces a number of progressions—a history of literary styles, embryological development, and the history of ideas regarding contraception, masturbation, birth, and death, to name but a few. Previously uncharted, however, is yet another historical development specifically outlined by Joyce in the Oxen chapter of *Ulysses*—that of the progression and consequent mutation of the genealogical patronymic. In Oxen, Joyce illustrates through mimicry and parody the corruption of the Irish patronymic throughout history, throughout politics, and throughout the various phonetic changes of the English language.

The chapter begins with a cluster of words that looks deceptively like a name—Deshil Holles Eamus (14.01)—but the first "real" names come two paragraphs later with the introduction of the *O'Shiels*, the *O'Hickeys* and the *O'Lees* (14.37)—names that illustrate the Irish clans' or septs' adoption of the *O'* prefix. The chapter closes with the nineteenth-century Negro *Massa Pat* designation (14.1557) for Paddy Dignam, and the modern blasphemous expletive "Christicle" (14.1579), which seems to refer ambiguously to Stephen Dedalus. In the chapter's chronological progression of names, Joyce inscribes the history of nomenclature from as early as the tenth century to the present day, outlining a pattern of genealogical development that parallels the chapter's other charted progressions. Birth, of course, is this chapter's theme, and Joyce takes the reader of Oxen from the conception of the Irish hereditary surname to the present day, where pseudonyms and bogus *O*'s can be acquired for a song.

Although the pattern of changed, truncated, and Anglicized names complements, on the one hand, the literary parodies contained in Oxen, the progression Joyce delineates is both inherently genealogical—that is, outside of literary history or popular literary influence—and inherently Irish, since, as we shall see, the names of characters in Oxen move from clan names to names that contain the *Mac* and *O'* that are characteristic of Boru's reign, to Roman, to Norman and French, to Anglo and Protestant, and to present-day pseudonyms. In short, the pattern of the names in Oxen mirrors the pattern of Irish political and genealogical history.

Ira Nadel suggests that Joyce's sensitivity to names and naming stems from his awarenesss of genealogical history, a history Joyce often incorporates in his fiction. In *Joyce and the Jews*, for example, Nadel comments on the historical handling of Nora Barnacle's family name, and credits her patronymical history with stirring Joyce's onomastic interests:

> In the late sixteenth and early seventeenth centuries, it became mandatory for the Irish to use English forms of their names. The need by non-Irish speakers to record the names of Irish people and places in legal documents was the reason. Gaelic names had to be transposed into English as was Nora Barnacle's. Originally O'Cadhain, pronounced *kyne*, the O was often dropped. Cadhain, Gaelic for barnacle goose (it was once thought such geese emerged from barnacle shells rather than eggs) quickly became translated into Barnacle. Nora may have told Joyce this background which would have naturally fascinated him; Barnacle appears twice in *Ulysses* (3.478; 15.4669) and *Finnegans Wake* (399.10; 423.22). (145)

When *barnacle* appears in *Ulysses* and *Finnegans Wake*, the word is a disguised onomastic pun,[3] evidence of Joyce's authorial impulse of nominal reference. In chapter 5, I discuss this type of self-conscious reflexivity as it relates to Joyce's works, as well as its occurrence in the works of writers like Derrida, Genet, Ponge, Shakespeare, and Donne. Joyce's use of nominal puns constitutes another element of his onomastic play and here, as in other passages, Joyce's disguised play is grained in history, specifically onomastic history.

Nowhere is such historical fashioning and retelling more evident than in the Oxen of the Sun episode of *Ulysses*, where Joyce executes his usual, deliberate foolery with names; but the way in which he classifies, truncates, emphasizes, and repeats with a difference each patronymic or surname is illustrative of the theme of the chapter; the way in which the patronymics gradually change indicates the pattern of alterations usually associated with a family's name during the course of its genealogical history.

The interwoven themes of name and birth particularly suit *Ulysses*'s

Oxen, since the Irish, specifically, have always had a special relationship to surnames. From the clan days, Irish surnames have always designated clan, family, ancestry, and topography; indeed, such identifications were important to the clan systems of early Ireland since lineage invariably led to kingships and provincial ownerships. In fact, the *O'* prefix, so often appended to the Irish surname, stems from the Gaelic *O'* or *ua*, the Irish word for grandson or, more loosely, male descendants. Notwithstanding, as noted earlier, many Irish popularly maintain that High King of Ireland Brian Boru, who reigned from A.D. 976 to 1014, "invented" the tradition of hereditary surnames (MacLysaght 62; Briffault 94). J. Anderson Black explains Boru's important patronymical contribution in *Your Irish Ancestors:*

> Brian's most important contribution was neither military nor political but the establishment of hereditary surnames. Surnames had been used in Ireland before this time but on a random basis; Brian made them compulsory. He is also credited with having introduced patronymics, i.e., *Mac,* meaning son of, and *O',* meaning descendent [sic] of. From now on lines of descent became increasingly easy to trace, and the great Irish names of today O'Brien, O'Connor, O'Rourke, MacCarthy and scores of others, were established for the first time. (45)

Whether the Irish did or did not, in fact, invent the hereditary surname is not so important as the fact that they claim to have done so—especially since a considerable number of Irish people did not use the hereditary surname even as late as 1650, according to the census taken in that year (J. Anderson Black 21). Consequently, the paucity of references to Boru in *Ulysses* is surprising in a text that relies so heavily on names and playful nomenclature. In Cyclops alone, as already noted, Bloom and three others are ironically afforded mock chieftain status when the Boruvian prefix *O'* is affixed to their names (12.216, 12.290, 12.374, 12.1183). The gratuitous *O*'s do not surface, however, in Oxen, and neither does Boru; but he is mentioned four times in *Ulysses:* once in the title of a public house (6.453), once in the catalogue of sea stones on the Citizen's girdle (12.177), and twice in the Ithaca chapter in reference to the title of a song that Bloom never completed (17.419, .433). Apparently supplanted by contemporary Irish patriots like Parnell, O'Connell, and Tone, Boru receives scanty press in the Dublin of 16 June 1904. Yet his influence is present if only in Joyce's maneuverings of patronymics and onomastics in the novel.

What Joyce does with names in Oxen is similar, at least in one way, to what Proust does with names in his novels. Roland Barthes writes of the Proustian name, "What is imitated [in the names] is of course not in Nature but in history, yet a history so old that it constitutes the language which has resulted from it as a veritable nature, the source of models and reasons" (65). This is exactly what Joyce does to the patronymic and surname in Oxen: his deliberate corruption of the names forms an historical pattern that reveals the evolved formation of names which, left unexamined, simply seem natural. In the simplest of terms, Ireland has been subject to invasion by the Norman-French and the Cambro-Normans or, as they are more usually called, the Anglo-Normans (MacLysaght 14); these resulted in an amalgam of settlers taking subsequent position or residence in Ireland. A multifarious assortment of surnames, then, can be found and traced not only in Ireland but in *Ulysses* as well because of Joyce's painstaking verisimilitude in that text. Joyce's boast that one could reconstruct the city of Dublin using *Ulysses* as a guide works well here, since one could also re-create its populace and its history using *Ulysses* as a surrogate for *Thom's Directory*. From the disunited Ireland of the Celts, to the intrusion of the Danes and Normans, through the years of English ascendency, to the upsurge of Irish nationalism and Irish letters after 1800—all these are critically and engagingly recorded in Joyce's nomenclature; his manipulation of onomastics supports the narrative, thematic, and historical patterns in his works.

What isolates and distinguishes Joyce's play with names in Oxen from the way he plays with names in the other seventeen chapters of *Ulysses*, or even throughout the rest of his works, is that in Oxen not only do the names inform us of personality, lineage, descent, breeding, and nationality, as they do in the earlier chapters of *Ulysses* (Haines's conspicuously non-Irish name suggests an Anglo-Norman descent, and Bloom's name reveals his racial family history, for example); but the names often indicate dissembling on the part of one or more characters, as in the case of Crotthers, who pretends to a Scottish heritage. Subsequently, the names serve to identify the affectations of the characters gathered in "Horne's Hall" and evolve into tightly packaged patro-charactonyms.

Oxen contains an assortment of puzzles for the genealogist interested in surnames. Since most surnames have their origin in one of four sources—place-names, nicknames, trade names, and patronymics—a person might be known by a variety of names in her or his lifetime; it is the reader's job to figure out what names belong to which characters. One of the minor puzzles in Oxen, for example, is figuring out who is Scottish and who is not, since that information helps the reader in pairing a particular name with a particular character. At various points, the text seems to afford Scottish status to the triumvirate of Lynch, Crotthers, and Bannon; that is, phrases like "a Scots fellow" seem to modify the names of the character they follow, as in "Vin. Lynch, a Scots fellow," for example (14.506), when, in fact, they do not: "a Scots fellow" is Joyce's description of the next person in the series, not an appositive to "Vin. Lynch," and it refers to Crotthers, identified at 14.191 as "one from Alba Longa," Scotland. Descriptive phrases of nationality usually replace names rather than modify them—and this compounds the reader's anguish. Equally confusing, however, is that the surnames of *Bannon* and *Crotthers* are not listed in George F. Black's *Surnames of Scotland*, even though these two characters are described in the chapter as Scots. In fact, the only Scottish surname in Oxen belongs to "Walking Mackintosh of lonely canyon" (14.1552–1553)—"*Macintosh* being the correct form of the name notwithstanding the intrusive *k*" (George F. Black 832). Curious to our understanding of the enigmatic M'Intosh is P. H. Reaney's analysis of the name in his *Dictionary of British Surnames*, where he identifies *M'Intosh* with the Scottish Gaelic *Mac an toisich*, meaning Son of the Chieftain (210).

In *Who's He When He's at Home* Shari and Bernard Benstock identify Crotthers as a Scottish medical student, but they do not identify Bannon with the Scots (31, 73), though he is described as follows in Oxen:

> Here the listener who was none other than the Scotch student, a little fume of a fellow, blond as tow, congratulated in the liveliest fashion with the young gentleman [Buck Mulligan] and, interrupting the narrative at a salient point, having desired his visavis with a polite beck to have the obligingness to pass him a flagon of cordial waters at the same time . . . asked the narrator as plainly as was ever done in words if he might treat him with a cup of it. (14.738–46)

After thanking the narrator for the goblet, Bannon slicks his hair, opens his bosom, pops out his locket containing Milly's photograph, and proceeds to tell Maledicty (Mulligan) of his coquette (14.752–66)—a tale he had promised to tell him earlier when they "chanced against" each other in the street (14.497).

Here, "the Scotch Student" is undoubtedly Bannon; it is he who is "congratulated in the liveliest fashion with the young gentleman," Mulligan, because everyone thinks Bannon is a partner in Mulligan's Omphalos scheme, since Mulligan begins passing out his business cards immediately after their entrance together. Additionally, prior to his entry into the hospital, Mulligan is described as "a gentleman's gentleman" (14.495); thenceforward, the term *gentleman* is usually given in reference to him, and he is talked about in gentlemanly terms, as in "the primrose elegance and townbred manners of Malachi Roland St John Mulligan" (14.1212–1213).

Adding to the confusion is the fact that Crotthers—undeniably a Scottish student, as he is called a number of times in the chapter—is identified as "one from Alba Longa, one Crotthers." While the Alba reference at once connects Crotthers with Scotland (*Alba* being the Gaelic name for Scotland), the Alba Longa reference connects him as well with the ancient Roman city of Latium, and not unequivocally with the Scottish. Moreover, since Latium is the birthplace of famed twins Romulus and Remus, the Alba Longa reference suggests a duality on the part of Crotthers; and given Joyce's interest in twins, and the evidence of his extensive knowledge of the mythology of twins in *Finnegans Wake*, Crotther's birthplace is important to our understanding of his lineage, if, indeed, the reader is meant to recall Rome's antagonistic twins. James Frazer reports in *The Golden Bough* that in ancient Latium the family name was transmitted through women instead of through men, and succession to the kingship in Rome and probably in Latium was transmitted in the female line (152). The name *Crotthers*, then, may actually be a matronymic. Notwithstanding these complications, the name *Crotthers* is not a Roman name, either; it is a variant of the Scottish surname *Carruthers*, "from the lands of Carruthers in the parish of Middlebie Dumfriesshire, in local speech pronounced Cridders" (G. Black 138; Reaney 61, 83). Crotthers, as the name appears in *Ulysses* with its uncharacteristic double *t*'s, seems like an Irishman's bungled phonetic attempt to reproduce the common, local *Cridders* pronunciation. The name *Crotthers* alone, then, has an implied heritage, an affected heritage, and an unspoken, hidden, and true heritage. By proclaiming to be Scottish, indeed, by dressing like one in Highland garb (14.1204–1205), Crotthers can fool all but the genealogists.

Yet names are rarely to be trusted in *Ulysses*, as they are often "impostures," functioning like sounds to trigger false associations, false allegiances, and false correspondences (*Crotthers* sounds more dignified than *Cridders,* for instance). Costello's name causes his companions to question his lineage, for example, but he defends his parentage saying,

> he was as good a son of the true fold as ever drew breath. Stap my vitals, said he, them was always the sentiments of honest Frank Costello which I was bred up most particular to honour thy father and thy mother that had the best hand to a rolypoly or a hasty pudding as you ever see what I always looks back on with a loving heart. (14.840–44)

In this passage, we are to identify "honest Frank Costello" as Frank "Punch" Costello's father. It is ironic, then, that a churl like Punch would be named after such an "honest" man—but we have been warned: names are impostures, and they account in no way for destiny. Of course, we are told that honest Frank, Punch's father the head-borough, "shed a pint of tears as often as he saw him," recalling Simon Dedalus's familial refrain, "Jesus wept: and no wonder, by Christ!" (3.68–69). We wonder, then, with the rest of Punch's companions, whether he is, in fact, "a son of the true fold" (14.840). After Punch is quieted by nurse Quigley, his friends upbraid him, hurling at him a host of insults that belie Costello's self-pronounced descent: "thou chuff, thou puny, thou got in peasestraw, thou losel, thou chitterling, thou spawn of a rebel, thou dykedropt, thou abortion thou . . . like a curse of God ape" (14.327–30). Similarly, Bloom later becomes repulsed by Costello, and when he makes a connection between Costello and Richard III, the reader envisions a Costello whose soul is as deformed as his body, an image that might cause the reader to question Costello's legitimacy regardless of whatever surname is evident in his signature. Bloom thinks,

> But the word of Mr Costello was an unwelcome language for him for he nauseated the wretch that seemed to him a cropeared creature of a mis-shapen gibbosity, born out of wedlock and thrust like a crookback toothed and feet first into the world, which the dint of the surgeon's pliers in his skull lent indeed a colour to, so as to put him in thought of that missing link of creation's chain desiderated by the late ingenious Mr Darwin. . . . he would concede neither to bear the name nor to herit the tradition of a proper breeding. (14.853–68)

The significance of the *Costello* name is further compounded by the fact that Costello was the first Norman family in Ireland to assume a "Mac" name, thus, appending the prefix signifying "son of" to their name (J. Black 160–61). This, of course, is the crux of the issue here, so far as

Costello is concerned. Who *is* he a son of, everyone in Horne's hospital wonders. In a chapter so belabored with birth imagery, so teeming with parturition, who is responsible for the birth of this "misshapen gibbosity"? All these questions, inspired by the encoded name *Costello*, conspire to assault the reader, who must not only try to piece together fragments of each character's drunken dialogue but identify, as well, each character's parentage and nationality.

Joyce may have been familiar with the significance of the *Costello* name since he was such an avid reader of the weekly *Irish Times* column "Irish Family Names." While many of the names in *Ulysses* are those of actual Dublin residents, the surnames Joyce created *ex nihilo*—divorced, for the moment, from their "duplication, accretion, modification, comic variation, and ironic juxtaposition" (Benstocks *Who's He* 1)—these usually pack three, four, five explicit contradictory messages, as in the names of *Crotthers* and *Costello* alone. Consequently, not usually one to mince words, Joyce does exactly that in Oxen—a chapter of *Ulysses* where he doesn't seem to spare words at all. In a chapter so embellished with flowery, ornate, and overemphasized language, Joyce practices a unique sort of economy in his naming of the characters: if a picture can be worth a thousand words, so, too, can a patronymic or surname.

While names can contain a number of unarticulated messages, the messages are not always consolatory. Bloom, for example, is told by one of the narrators of the episode, "No, Leopold. Name and memory solace thee not" (14.1074). Bloom, of course, has no *real* name to solace him, since by deedpoll his father changed the family name from Virag to Bloom (17.1866–1867). Bloom's surname is a fraud, and his uneasiness about his name finds its way into later narratives; that is, nearly every time Bloom's father is mentioned from the Circe episode on, he is referred to as Rudolph Bloom, but his Virag identity is characteristically parenthesized, as in "Rudolph Bloom (born Virag)."[4] In Circe, Bloom muses on the etymological similarities between the names *Virag*, *Bloom*, and *Flower*. Holding Martha Clifford's flower in his hand, Bloom connects the yellow blossom to his real and self-created surnames:

BLOOM
(*produces from his heartpocket a crumpled yellow flower*) This is the flower in question. It was given me by a man I don't know his name. (*plausibly*) You know that old joke, rose of Castile. Bloom. The change of name. Virag. (15.737–41)

Importantly, Bloom puns on the semantic similarities between the surnames *Virag* and *Bloom* when he recalls Lenehan's paronomastic joke.
Just as Lenehan fuses the title of the opera *Rose of Castile* with "rows of
cast steel," the name *Bloom*, like the self-generated *Flower*, puns on
Virag—not homophonically but semantically.

Virag's unexplained and seemingly spontaneous change of name is
suggested in the Irish bull section of Oxen, where lord Harry (Henry
VIII) changes his name after leafing through a chapbook:

> on picking up a blackthumbed chapbook that he kept in the pantry he
> found sure enough that he was a lefthanded descendant of the famous
> champion bull of the Romans, *Bos Bovum*, which is good bog Latin for
> boss of the show. After that, says Mr Vincent, the lord Harry put his head
> into a cow's drinkingtrough in the presence of all his courtiers and pull-
> ing it out again told them all his new name. (14.626–32)

Because it is the female's, the cow's drinking trough that seems to be
the instrument for the name change, perhaps the parallel is that Virag's
marriage played an important role in the patronymical change. Gifford
identifies the allusion here to Irish-born Anne Boleyn. Divorce and marriage to her resulted in Henry VIII's turning from the Pope and assuming a new name, "Defender of the Faith" (Gifford 425). Curiously, lord
Harry's "research" reveals that he is a left-handed descendant of the
bull, and since left-handedness is emphasized at the very beginning of
the Circe episode—"Kithogue!" being one of the first words of dialogue there (15.18)—the left-handed line of descent is important to our
understanding of lord Harry's, Virag's, and Bloom's lineage. Later in
Circe, Bloom muses on the size and proportion of his left hand, saying
that it "calls for more effort. Why? Smaller from want of use" (15.670–
71). Bloom's comparison of his left hand with his right suggests a reference to masturbation, but more likely, Bloom is referring to the size and
proportion of his family tree. Since Bloom, like his father, Virag, is a
descendant of the left-hand side of the family tree (traditionally the side
afforded the patriarchy in a printed text or "chapbook," i.e., the *verso*
leaf), then his left is, indeed, smaller from want of use since he deliberately has not completed intercourse with Molly for some eleven years.[5]
In lord Harry's case, left-handedness many also suggest the "sinister,"
since Henry VIII's assumption of theocratic power was, from a Catholic
point of view, not right.

One of the antagonistic narrators of Oxen condemns Bloom for his lack of regeneration, saying, "Has he not nearer home a seedfield that lies fallow for the want of the ploughshare?" (14.929–30)—in fact, the very seed that might sow the metaphorical field is wasted, like Onan's in Bloom's Nausicaa masturbation. The name change, then, signals for Bloom not only the end of the Virag patriarchy, but the impending end of the Bloom patriarchy—the left side of the family tree—the guilt for which particularly haunts Bloom, especially since his only son died shortly after birth.

Yet so far as Stephen might be concerned, having one's name changed from Virag to Bloom is still not so bad as having a low or common name to begin with, as indeed, *Bloom* is not a noticeably common name in Ireland though Louis Hyman manages to identify dozens of Blooms in *The Jews of Ireland* (169–76). If we recall Stephen's sharp assessment of the names of Father *Dolan* and Father *Moran* in *A Portrait* (55, 221), we realize that Stephen might have made the same assessment of the surname *Lynch*, since that name is among the hundred most common names in Ireland (J. Black 202).

In *Your Irish Ancestors*, Black reports that the name *Lynch* is of dual origin: "it can be traced back to the native Gaelic name O'Loignsigh and also to the Norman name de Lench" (202). Though it is not certain whether Joyce knew the Gaelic for *Lynch*, O'Loignsigh is indeed a titillating subtext for a name that curiously appears for the first time in the Oxen episode, where Mina Purefoy's loins are, no doubt, sighing under the strain of her three-day labor. Here, Joyce exploits the visual joke in the orthography of the name. Yet both the Gaelic *O'* and the Norman *de* indicate a well-established ancestry for Lynch—Irish or French— since both prefixes suggest that he is a "descendant of." But the more usual Norman prefix in that sense is *Fitz*, and *de* generally indicates the place from which a family comes (e.g., medieval French writers Jean de Meung, Chrétien de Troyes—from the towns of Meung and Troyes respectively). The surname *Lynch*, then, is neither unequivocally Gaelic nor unequivocally Norman; in fact, Samuel Brown further complicates its geneaology by suggesting that Lynch is an "English name derived from the Old English *hlinc*, meaning hill" (205). Lynch, however, seems to know where he comes from, or where he'd like to come from: he affects a French dispositionand because of this, two "French" names are generated for him: *Mr Cavil*, from the Old French *cavalier*, and *Monsieur Lynch* (U 14.468, 14.784). Consequently, the affected Frenchness of a number of the students in the common room invades the narrative, and soon everyone is a *monsieur* and Mulligan is *Le Fécondateur* (14.778), a reference to his proposed fertilizing farm.

In addition, the name *Lynch* is often connected with the name *Joyce*, since *Joyce* and *Lynch* are associated with the fourteen Tribes of Galway, "an appellation that was invented as a term of opprobrium by the Cromwellian forces who regarded unfavourably the close bond of friendship and relationship between the chief families of the city" (MacLysaght 49). Though a term of contempt, the families afterward adopted the appellation as a mark of distinction. Apart from the Joyces and the Lynches, the rubric Tribes of Galway includes, as well, these twelve families, although some authorities omit the name *Deane* and prefer to list only thirteen (see MacLysaght 49n): *Athy, Blake, Bodkin, Browne, Deane, Darcy, Fant, French, Kirwan, Martin, Morris,* and *Skerrett*. Of the fourteen Tribes of Galway, it is interesting that Joyce makes good use of the names *Athy, Bodkin, Browne, Joyce,* and *Lynch* in his works, making the name *Athy* the subject of discussion in the Clongowes infirmary in *A Portrait*, for example:

> —You have a queer name, Dedalus, and I have a queer name too, Athy. My name is the name of a town. . . .
> —Can you answer me this one? Why is the county Kildare like the leg of a fellow's breeches?
> Stephen thought what could be the answer and then said:
> —I give it up.
> —Because there is a thigh in it, he said. Do you see the joke? Athy is the town in the county Kildare and a thigh is the other thigh.
> —O, I see, Stephen said.
>
> (25)

Joyce also makes *Bodkin* not only the renamed subject of his story in "The Dead," but he continually puns on the names *Furey* and *Bodkin*. Glasheen pointed out in an early entry for *Bodkin* that "Joyce steadily plays on Furey-Furies and Hamlet's bare bodkin" in the *Wake* (*Second Census* 31). Joyce also puns incessantly on another Tribes of Galway name in his limitless versions of the name *Browne* in the *Wake*. A Mr. Browne also appears in "The Dead" as one of the Morkan's guests who, in fact, calls particular attention during the course of the dinner to his name when he says, "—Well, I hope, Miss Morkan, . . . that I'm brown enough for you because, you know, I'm all brown" (*D* 200). Such self-conscious references to one's own surname make it all the more curious that Joyce rarely "hid his own name, a fair name," in his works, especially since he makes good use of the names of the Tribes of Galway throughout his writings. Except for its few appearances in the *Wake*, where it is a composite made from the names of two or more people, the surname *Joyce* is conspicuous by its absence elsewhere.

Apart from Browne, Bodkin, Athy, and Joyce, however, the Lynches were the most influential of the "Tribes," as no fewer than eighty-four mayors of Galway were of the Lynch family during the 170-year period beginning in 1484 "when Dominick Lynch procured the city's charter from Richard III" and ending in 1654 "when Catholics were debarred from civic offices" (MacLysaght 213). Joyce's reason for including the tribesman among the Oxen debauchees and libertines may have been guided by verisimilitude since *Lynch* is, indeed, a common surname in Ireland. He may have used the name *Lynch*, though, with the hope of triggering the father/son association that would have been so familiar to his Irish audience, and it is this association that angered Joyce's friend Cosgrave in 1905, prompting him to threaten Joyce with a libel action when he was called *Lynch* in *Stephen Hero* (*Letters* 2:103), since the name associated him with James fitz Stephen Lynch, a Galway mayor who in 1493 hanged his own son in Market Street. MacLysaght explains the allusive name as follows:

> Of all the Galway Lynches the one most likely to be remembered by any visitor to that city is James Lynch, the stern mayor who in 1493 felt it his duty to hang his own son for an offence for which the penalty was death: the spot where the event took place, known as the gate of the Old Jail, with its tragic inscription, is still pointed out and retold. (213)

This story of filicide ill befits the theme of birth that Joyce attributes to the Oxen episode; yet the father's hanging of the son functions as another "crime . . . against fecundity" (*Letters* 1:139); and although it is not exactly an act that "steriliz[es] the act of coition" (*Letters* 1:139), like the condom or prophylactic, it can be called in similar terms, a "Killchild" (*U* 14.467). Because the topics of birth, fathers, sons, and death are prominent not only in all of *Ulysses* but especially in Oxen, the story of James Lynch is important to our understanding of Vincent Lynch and of his appearance in the Oxen episode. To be sure, Lynch's presence in the chapter is essential, since it is he who scolds Stephen about his scant literary production, calling Stephen's output a "capful of light odes" and reminding him of the name his friends had for him years ago, *Stephaneforos* (*U* 14.1121; *P* 168).

Joyce inscribes in the nomenclature of Oxen the Norman-French invasion of Ireland, the Roman influence, and the Anglo infiltration; but interestingly enough, he indicates the Anglo presence in the name of one who is arguably the most important character in the episode—the "Young hopeful" (*U* 14.1333–1334), the new baby Purefoy, who will be christened *Mortimer Edward* "after the influential third cousin of Mr Purefoy in the Treasury Remembrancer's office, Dublin Castle" (14.1334–1336). Of course, the names of all the Purefoy children are important—as is their surname *pure faith*—since their given names, like their surname, indicate their Anglo-Protestantism; but the birth of a child, a son, a "hoopsa boyaboy" (14.5), is important because it signals rebirth and regeneration for the race: it increases the left-hand side of the family tree. In an episode where Joyce illustrates the corruption of the patronymic the defilement and degeneration of the Name, we might look to the naming of the new child as one of the most important acts in the episode. As names do, Mortimer Edward's name will shape his identity; no doubt, that is why he is named after Purefoy's "influential" third cousin. Mortimer Edward may have his name changed like *Virag*, altered like *"Beau Mount and Lecher"* (14.356), corrupted from *Dr John Alexander Dowie* into *"Alexander J Christ Dowie"* (14.1584), truncated like *"Patk. Dignam"* (14.474) and *"Mullee!"* (14.1453), ornamented like *MacCostello*, or disregarded and displaced by a nickname like *"Punch"* Costello or *"Buck"* Mulligan. Inherent in its treatment of the history of nomenclature, Oxen contains a lesson for the little Mortimer: Joyce is preparing the Purefoy's little lump of love not only for the days to come but for the names to come.

Joyce's use of names, however, is not limited to his knowledge of genealogical history, as many times Joyce will corrupt historical data including names to protect his own superstitious beliefs, as Patrick A. McCarthy explains in *"Ulysses": Portals of Discovery*:

> The way similar names seem to imply guilt by association is indicated not only in Molly's dislike of Moll Flanders but also in the fact that whenever Bloom thinks about the Phoenix Park murders case he is either wrong (5.378–82; 16.1053–54) or uncertain (8.442–43) about the first name of the informer, James Carey, possibly because James Joyce wants to avoid any personal association with an informer. (125)

Just as Joyce drops the given name *James* from the string of names he attributes to Endymion, changing Farrell's Christian name in *Ulysses* from *James* to *Cashel* to avoid any personal association with a man who was, not incidentally, a lunatic, Joyce takes the same onomastic liberty with the informer Carey. Joyce had an unabashed superstition about names; he saw them as omens, often repeating to friends, for example, that "one hopeful sign was that Penelope was a weaver, like his English benefactress," Harriet (R. Ellmann 517). Names were charged, he believed; they were magical, portentous, and propitious. The beliefs to which Joyce held fast in life animated his use of names in fiction. He often created unarticulable and symbiotic bonds between names and characters, solidifying a nominal appropriateness in his fiction that Plato's Cratylus would have applauded, and intimating patterns of history that trace the thought, culture, and existence of humanity.

The task, however, of inscribing a nominal or genealogical historicity in fiction is a difficult one, as most available genealogical documents have been destroyed. In *The Mountain of Names: A History of the Human Family*, Alex Shoumatoff discusses one of the many disheartening statistics that thwarts onomastic research:

> Of all the people ever alive, between eighty-five and ninety-two percent lived, died, and slipped into complete oblivion without even leaving their names. The loss of their identities, like the extinction of a species, is irreparable. There is no "catalogue of catalogues" such as Jorge Luis Borges has written of, in which we might hope to find the names of everybody who has lived. Such records as were kept of human populations in the past were ravaged by various agents of destruction. The Black Death of 1360, for instance, not only killed half the people in London; [but] fires set to fumigate the victims' quarters destroyed many of the documents with which they and their ancestors could have been identified (249–50)

Doubtless, Joyce was aware of the lack of documentation of the human race, since he suggests in the *Wake* that we should be grateful for what written records we have: "and, sure, we ought really to rest thankful at this deleteful hour of dungflies dawning we have even a written on with dried ink scrap of paper at all to show for ourselves, tare it or leaf it . . . after all that we lost and plundered of it . . . cling to it as with drowning hands," he writes (*FW* 118.31–119.03).

Joyce often reminded readers and publishers that his fiction chronicled the age, that his writings were a sort of historical fiction chronicling the attitudes and conscience of his race. The reader leaves Stephen Dedalus at the end of *A Portrait* as he goes out to "encounter for the millionth time the reality of experience and to forge in the smithy of [his] soul the uncreated conscience of [his] race" (253). In *Ulysses*, that is precisely what Joyce has done: he has architecturalized the life of Dublin, turning "history" and "conscience" onto an urban landscape, writing an account of a city and its populace, and inscribing forever the physical labyrinth wrought by Daedalus.

Shoumatoff continues in a depressing litany that lists the many natural destructions of ancestral lineage papers,[6] what Joyce called "the reducing of records to ashes" (*FW* 189.35–36); but Shoumatoff's is a wonderful compilation of historical genealogical data and an invaluable sourcebook about nominal investigation. He explains that

> the age of modern vital record keeping is widely considered to have begun in 1538, when Thomas Cromwell, Henry VIII's Vicar General, ordered the parish clergy to enter on books every christening, wedding, and burial. . . . Some of the 10,894 ancient parishes in England and Wales did not begin their registers until 1700, but most of the other European countries, following the British example, had started to keep parish registers by the end of the sixteenth century. (252)

While *Ulysses* is clearly Joyce's urban and architectural rendering of Dublin, *Finnegans Wake*, I would like to suggest, is his rendering of the race, his approximation of Borges's "catalogue of catalogues"—not in the literal sense, that is, not a categorical listing upon listing of forgotten progeny; but *Finnegans Wake* can be mined for catalogues of historical names—biblical, Egyptian, Greek, Roman, Gothic, medieval—chains that reveal historical continuity and suggest, as well, that *Finnegans Wake* restores onomastic history just as *Ulysses* restores the Irish/Dublin part of that history. A repository of names and playful nomenclature, *Finnegans Wake* reconstructs Dublin not like *Ulysses*, "brick by brick," as Joyce suggested, but letter by letter, syllable by syllable, person by person, race by race.

The set piece of the Prankquean's Tale, for example, disguises references to a wealth of ancestral progeny. Beginning with references to Adam (*FW* 21.06) and Eve ("ribberrobber" 21.08), the passage also alludes to the Greek legend of Hilara (called Hilary here), the sister of Phoebe who was abducted by Castor and Pollux. The abduction of Hilara by the Greek twins fits nicely in the Prankquean's Tale since that is a tale of the abduction of Jarl van Hoother's twins, Tristopher and

Hilary. The names *Tristopher* and *Hilary* also pun aurally on Giordano
Bruno's motto, "*In tristitia hilaris hilaritate tristis*"—"in sadness cheer-
ful, in gaiety sad" (McHugh 21). The Bruno allusion, then, identifies an
Italian reference in the set piece. In addition, the names *Dermot* and
Grania are taken from the Finn myth, while the *Grace* of Grace O'Malley
resounds with the Irish *Grania* and *Grannuaile*, recorded in Joyce's tale
as "brannewail" (*FW* 21.25). Adaline Glasheen states in *Second Census*
that "Jarl van Hoother is Shakespeare, and his twin boys, Tristopher
and Hillary, are Tragedy and Comedy. The Prankquean is the Muse
who mixes up comedy and tragedy, as they are mixed up in Shakespeare's later plays" (193). Shakespeare, himself a father of twins, adds
more layers of meaning to the Tale and provides a literary context for
the names central to the Hilary and Tristopher passage. The references
to Cromwell as "cromcruwell" and to Brian Boru as "the old terror of
the danes" (*FW* 22.32), as well as the mentioning of Brodar, Boru's as-
sassin at Clontarf (22.02), steer the passage toward an historical context, shifting it from mythical and medieval literary courses. Further,
the reference to Strongbow—"the strength of his bowman's bill"
(23.02–03)—reinforces the historicity of the passage. Biblical names
abound, as well. Aside from the name of the gospeler Mark, Joyce includes another biblical allusion when he adds the name *Boanerges* to
Hoother, calling him "Jarl von Hoother Boanerges" (22.31–32), a reference to Mark's gospel 3:17: "Boanerges, which is, The sons of thunder"
(McHugh 22). The later allusions to the books of Job and Genesis also
help to mix biblical history with literary and political history in the
Prankquean's Tale. With such a wealth of races and literatures represented in the three-page tale, Joyce successfully reconstructs literature,
thought, history, and culture from the prelapsarian paradise of Adam
and Eve through the medieval, Greek, and Roman cultures to the present day.

Maintaining a fidelity to Joyce's literary and historical braggadocio—
in particular, to his oft-quoted boast that the city of Dublin could be
reconstructed from the pages of *Ulysses*—C. P. Curran discussed Joyce
and his writings in that light in his obituary of Joyce in the *Irish Times:*

> He contained Dublin. . . . If Dublin were destroyed, his words could
> rebuild the houses; if its population were wiped out, his books could
> repeople it. Joyce was many things, but he was certainly the last forty
> volumes of *Thom's Directory* thinking aloud. (Hart and Knuth 13)

Joyce's fidelity to the real surfaced not only in his fiction but in his literary criticism as well. He complained, for example, about George Moore's unrealistic portrayal of characters in *The Untilled Field*, arguing against the believability of a character's looking up a train timetable:

> I have read Moore's "Untilled Field" in Tauchnitz. Damned stupid. . . . A lady who had been living for three years on the line between Bray and Dublin is told by her husband that there is a meeting in Dublin at which he must be present. She looks up the table to see the hours of the train. This on D[ublin] W[icklow] and W[exford] R[ailway] where the trains go regularly: this after three years. Isn't it rather stupid of Moore. (*Letters* 2:71)

Apart from what he regarded as Moore's unbelievable character situations, though, Joyce thought Moore an admirable, albeit improvable, chronicler of the age.

Joyce also approved of Moore's playful nomenclature, even though he insisted on taking Moore's playfulness one step further, revealing a one-upmanship that would characterize Joyce's writings to his death and then some. McCarthy explains in "The Moore-Joyce Nexus" that Joyce may have enjoyed a laugh at the expense of Moore by revealing the elder author as the less inventive of the two:

> There are, as it happens . . . obvious allusions in *Ulysses* to [Moore's] *The Lake*, all of them dependent on our recognizing that Buck Mulligan, Stephen's roommate and rival, is based on Joyce's one-time friend, Oliver Gogarty. Moore's real reason for appropriating Gogarty's name for the protagonist of *The Lake* has not been satisfactorily explained. . . . Moore borrowed only Gogarty's name, not his character, and tried to smooth matters over by telling Mrs. Gogarty, "Madame supply me with two such joyous dactyls and I will gladly change the name"—a remark one critic credits with having inspired Mulligan's remark about his name [in the Telemachus episode]: "My name is absurd too: Malachi Mulligan, two dactyls." (110–11)[7]

While Joyce suggests to Stanislaus that Gogarty, "*O St Jesus*," might have "laughingly suggested" the name to Moore "for his greater glory" (*Letters* 2:163), McCarthy suggests that Joyce was motivated to invent the two-dactyl name by "professional jealousy, insecurity, and the memory of being ignored by Moore while he was in Dublin" ("Moore-Joyce Nexus" 99): these, McCarthy contends, "prevented Joyce from acknowledging a major literary debt" (99), but they also contributed to the one-upmanship that would characterize Joyce's literary revenge. Naming and revenge are issues I deal with below, in chapter 4; but for now, suffice it to say that Joyce created much of his fiction for his own "greater glory," in an effort to outdo other writers. Naming is but one of the forms in which he tries to outperform the competition—either by naming them directly or deforming their names in his works, or by "outnaming" them, by surpassing their onomastic inventiveness, as he did with Moore.

While many of Joyce's names contain blatant historical puns—such as the names *Rose Lankester* and *Blanche Yorke* of the Yawn chapter in *Finnegans Wake* (FW 485.12)—Joyce also uses names to suggest the history of humanity, the history of letters, and the history of warfare and politics. Just as *Finnegans Wake* is mimetic of the novel, names in the *Wake* are mimetic of history; they intimate historical patterns and reconstruct, for our greater glory, the history of humanity. In his rhetoric of names Joyce successfully merges literature with history, creating a system of nomenclature that functions not merely as aesthetics but as historical documentation. Part and parcel of his reconstructive boasts, the multiplicity of names in Joyce's texts accounts, in part, for lost history, for irreplaceable and irretrievable knowledge about the past. Of course, Joyce's reconstructive efforts are often amusing and self-promoting, and they often undercut the seriousness of such an endeavor. But if history is a nightmare, as Stephen suggests, then Joyce's manipulation of the dream is less frightening and surely less mawkish than one might suppose. His efforts are self-serving since they afford him the opportunity not only to inscribe history but to embellish it, to view it from a Cyclopean perspective, omitting details that compromise his versions of history and literature, and to rewrite it, an occasion to author and re-author, father and re-father the human race. Joyce's historical maneuverings allow him to usurp the role of the celebrated Muse of history, Clio, as well as the roles of her eight sisters, allowing him to be the ultimate creator and affording him an office much like God's own—creator, mixer, arranger—in a kind of alchemical processs of historical onomastics.

CHAPTER THREE

Naming and Gender

Matthew O'Connor in Djuna Barnes's *Nightwood* (1936) tells Nora "there is not one of us who, given an eternal incognito, a thumbprint nowhere set against our souls, would not commit rape, murder and all abominations" (88). He is right—not only in the pragmatic sense, that our lack of anonymity makes cowards of us all, that our names identify us and would link us unwittingly to the abominations we would, name-less, commit, but also in the sense that names *fix* our identities. Names prescribe and maintain our behavior, freezing in time and space our personalities; and because names can both order and stifle, codify and smother, characters in a fiction often rebel against such nominal system-atization. "To be named is to undergo reification," Susan Cohen ar-gues, and she adds that characters, particularly female characters, re-ject any such occulting (793). In this chapter, I discuss how Joyce's women characters not only mutiny against their names but manipu-late, truncate, and violate the names of others to mete out a particularly literary and rhetorical revenge against the patriarchal constructs of naming in Victorian Dublin. I focus my discussion on Joyce's women, but because Stephen practices a similar revenge in Scylla and Charyb-dis, where he contemptuously names and renames his audience, changing, truncating, and mutilating their names to match his assess-ment of their characters and wits, my discussion of literary and rhetori-cal revenge carries over into the next chapter, a discussion of the Dedalian mode of nominal sedition.

Naming is a legacy of male tradition. In Genesis, one of the earliest myths of naming and creation, Adam was the first namer. As Joyce envisioned the prelapsarian scene, it was a form of "crudities to ani-mals for he had put his own nickelname on every toad, duck and her-ring . . . of the park" (*FW* 505.36–506.03). Adam's nominal execution also has been re-created by John Milton in Book 8 of *Paradise Lost*. In Milton's analysis, the act of naming is not only one of privilege, one of power, one of domination, but one of apprehension as well, an act that presumes an instant comprehension of the thing named. The authority of personality, then, as well as the authority of evaluation, rests with the namer; and when such authorities reside as they do with patriarchy, the woman character often rejects it. Joyce unveils this particularly female concern in his writings.

Because the power to name has rested since Adam with patriarchy, the female's position is doubly fixed—not only by a name that declares her gender but by one that bespeaks her male-defined identity. For a woman, the patronymic is always a borrowed name; it is always an "imposture," as Stephen notes in Eumaeus (*U* 16.362–63). It is either the name of the father or the name of the husband. Men have accepted the permanency of their names as one of the rights of being male, but women's names carry no such permanency. It is customary and usual for a woman to surrender her surname when she marries—shedding for once the name of the father—but it is not unusual for a woman to lose her proper name, her first name, as well, since she is subsequently referred to in feminized constructs of her husband's name, as in *Mrs. Donnelly* of "Clay," and *Mrs. Yelverton Barry* and *Mrs. Denis Breen* of *Ulysses*, for example. (A notable exception occurs in "A Painful Case," when we learn Mrs. Sinico's first name, *Emily*, only after her death [*D* 113], and only in relation to the identification of her body.) The name of a married woman, then, has only one marker that distinguishes it from her husband's name, one marker that indicates that she is *not* her husband, and that is the title *Mrs.* Any name acquired through marriage, then, identifies the woman in terms of what she is not. Linguistically and semantically, the title *Mrs.* acts as a marker to identify what is *not* there: since the title *Mrs.* has always declared gender, when placed before the name of the husband, *Mrs.* declares the absence of the phallus since it feminizes the name that follows. The wife becomes, by name, an inferiorized version of her husband, a Mrs. Him. She shares his identical name, but she is forever diminished because the name is not her own. Thus, the married woman metamorphoses into a forgery of the husband. The surname, then, like the patronymic, becomes a *prescriptive* name. It is patriarchy's way, as Matthew O'Connor explains to Nora in Barnes's *Nightwood*, of "dressing the unknowable in the garments of the known" (136).

In his discussion of naming in the first three stories in *Dubliners*, Fritz Senn suggests that a name is a means of "dressing the unknowable," that names act as drapery, and that they serve to evaluate and reevaluate the unfamiliar. Not coincidentally, Shem, the artist figure and projection of Joyce himself in *Finnegans Wake*, is described as "*Mr O'Shem the Draper*" (FW 421.25). The reference is to Jonathan Swift's *Drapier Letters*, in which Swift assumes the name of *Drapier*; but the play on *Drapier/Draper* is an interesting one, since the pseudonym functions as an example of nominal drapery. Senn explains that names, like drapery, are used in *Dubliners* as

> something assumed, put on, and sometimes changed. They are changed in the second story which features two adventurers. Only one of them is identified, and this with a touch of condescension: "a boy named Mahony" (*D* 21). He is a namer too: he "spoke of Father Butler as Bunsen Burner" (*D* 22). In the emergency of an unforseen encounter, an evasive plan is considered: "In case he [the strange man, doing something queer, but also never named] asks us for our names . . . let you be Murphy and I'll be Smith" (*D* 26). This type of pseudonymous drapery was introduced into Western literature by Odysseus of many counsels and of several aliases. What we deduce is that the narrator's name is *not* Smith. And pseudo-Smith will in fact cover his escape by calling "loudly across the field:—Murphy!" (*D* 28). From what we can tell, these final words, the last ones spoken, are those uttered with most volume within the story: they are an onomastic falsehood, a fiction within a fiction. . . . "An Encounter" is a story about the naming and renaming of Mahony and his reevaluation. There is nothing condescending anymore when Murphy becomes Mahony again in the last paragraph. (467)

Throughout life, our names often change because we are constantly being evaluated and reevaluated—our nominal identities move from parental nicknames, to childhood tag names, to adolescent counterparts, to adult names; and in between, each of us assumes and shrugs off a host of other generated names. Mary Seeman explains that the progressive evolution of a person's name is a cultural trademark, and she cites how personal patterns of naming can be "read," recalling that "a women's magazine once chronicled the development and transformation of a woman's affiliations by the successive names with which, over the years, she signed her letters: Judy; Judi; Judith; Jude; J.; Judy" ("Unconscious Meaning" 242). The multiple signatures recall the closing affixed by Anna Livia Plurabelle to one of her letters: "Your wife. Amn. Anm. Amm. Ann" (*FW* 495.33). Yet before they mature and invest their names with their personalities, women are the only creatures, save children, whose names are assigned and issued by social sanction; since roughly half these children are male, they, too, must be assigned and issued ill-fitting names by social sanction. This is the point that Lacan seems to be making by equating the "Name of the Father" with law, "entry into the Symbolic," and the ascension into language. To be assigned a patronymic family name, whether you're male or female, signifies one's entry into an already hierarchical signifying system and social order, and one's subservience to, straitjacketing by, a patriarchal system. It is society's sanction of patronymics that most diminishes the importance of women's names, something Clarissa Dalloway notes in Woolf's *Mrs. Dalloway* when she thinks of her own invisibility, saying, "this being Mrs. Dalloway; not even Clarissa anymore; this being Mrs. Richard Dalloway" (14). Patronymics, like spousal names, are an attempt to define or "eff" the ineffable; each name is an attempt to drape woman in familiar garments.

One way that women get around these issues is through self-naming—autonomastics—or through the use of a pseudonym. Both attempt to "rupture paternal origin," according to Brook Thomas, but the pseudonym, in particular, he says, "indicates a desire to lessen the control of others over us" (117). While a number of characters in Joyce, male and female, adopt false names, it is important that we distinguish the grounds that motivate women to create names for themselves from those that motivate men to do the same.

Women commonly are subject to a process of naming over which they have no control, since their behavior is so often subject to male scrutiny; but they often name themselves, too, and once women characters generate self-names, they rupture not only paternal bonds, but they sever the ties of identity that bind them. A woman might be moved to autonomastics, for example, because she dislikes her married name. Molly muses in Penelope over the horror of certain "awful names with a bottom in them Mrs Ramsbottom or some other kind of a bottom" (*U* 18.844–45). Apart from her dislike of *Ramsbottom*, Molly also considers some "devils queer" Gibraltar names, among them, the names *Pisimbo* and *Opisso*. Though scandalized by the micturitional name *Opisso*—Molly swears, "O what a name Id go and drown myself in the first river if I had a name like her O my" (18.1466–1467)—chances are that she doesn't recognize the *piss* in *Pisimbo*, since the *s* in that name would be pronounced as a *z*. The juxtapositioning of *Pisimbo* and *Opisso*, then, is most likely a successful element of Joyce's visual play.

Molly's attention to names is often humorous, particularly her assumption about how the writer Paul de Kock got his name. Molly conjectures, "Mr de Kock I suppose the people gave him that nickname going about with his tube from one woman to another" (18.969–70); but Molly's nominal critique also extends to her own name, which she dislikes. She complains that "my mother whoever she was might have given me a nicer name the Lord knows after the lovely one she had Lunita Laredo" (18.846–48). We can assume that Molly is thinking of her maiden name *Tweedy* here and not her given name *Marion*, since many of her thoughts in the passage are about her real and imaginable surnames: "I never thought that would be my name Bloom" (18.840–41), she thinks, though "its better than Breen or Briggs" (18.843–44). "Mulvey I wouldnt go mad about either" (18.845–46), Molly adds; and then she imagines, "suppose I divorced him [and became] Mrs Boylan" (18.846). Of course, this assumes that Molly thinks her mother could have given her a different family name; and since Molly was most likely illegitimate, her mother would have had a choice of family name, a choice that a married mother would not have. For example, Molly is no doubt remembering a *Mrs*. Opisso when she thinks of the Gibraltar woman with the scandalous family name, since she suggests that she'd have to drown herself to get rid of the name.

Molly's apparent dislike of the name *Tweedy* doesn't quite explain why she dislikes books with a Molly in them, though it is possible that she does not care for casual or familiar uses of the name by well-meaning neighbors or by irreverent novelists: "Molly bawn she gave me by Mrs Hungerford on account of the name," Molly thinks, adding, "I dont like books with a Molly in them like that one he brought me about the one from Flanders a whore always shoplifting anything she could cloth and stuff and yards of it" (18.656–59). Though the reader never learns of the genesis of the *Molly* name—that is, whether Molly invited the use of the name herself or whether it was given to her by someone else, a father, mother, girlfriend, boyfriend, lover—Molly's comment implies that she objects to having her name associated specifically with female characters "like that one" in Defoe's *Moll Flanders*, a shoplifter and a whore. To be sure, some readers see Molly's criticism extending elsewhere, suggesting that she dislikes the way in which women like herself are represented in male-authored books. More likely, Molly objects to the use of her name, a name from the Latin *mollis,* meaning "soft," a characteristic of Molly's to which Bloom refers many times throughout the day: "Body getting a bit softy. I would notice that: from remembering. . . . But the shape is there. The shape is there still. Shoulders. Hips. Plump" (6.204–7).

Like Molly, dozens of women in Joyce's fiction have nicknames or diminutives, names that are affectionate forms of endearment on the one hand, but somewhat character-deflating on the other hand, caricatures, almost, that suggest softness, smallness, sweetness, or frailty. In this respect, it is interesting that Molly's mother's name (a name that Molly likes, *Lunita Laredo*) translates into "small moon." And such onomastic "smallness" is passed through the female line from mother to daughter: the name *Marion* is a diminutive of *Mary;* the name *Milly,* a diminutive of *Millicent.* Indeed, Bloom even muses upon the similarities between the mother and daughter when he suggests, first, that their names, like their personalities, are the "same thing watered down" (6.87), and later when he recalls that they referred to Milly as "Marionette" (15.540). Both of the first names to which Molly responds (*Marion* and *Molly*) can be read as names that suggest a lack of strength and independence. Though the name *Milly* is taken from the name *Millicent,* which means "strong work," this meaning is contradicted when the name *Millicent* is rendered in the diminutive, since the name *Milly* deconstructs any suggestion of strength. Again, there is an onomastic association of the female with the weak in the diminutive form of her name. Consequently, any diminutive name of the woman defines her in patriarchally licensed terms: she is small, weak, frail, dependent, and, most important, like her mother. Naming in the diminutive, in other words, is one way of ensuring female oppression. Regardless of whether the name is given to the woman or whether it is self-adopted, there are semantic and associational differences between diminutives assigned to and adopted by women and those assigned to and adopted by men, as we shall see.

To be sure, in Ireland diminutive naming is also common with male names—*Paddy* for *Patrick,* for example, or *Shauneen* (little Sean) for *Sean;* moreover, the Irish distinguish between fathers and sons with the same name by adding *Beag* (little) or *Mor* (big) to the name, as in *Seamus Beag,* or *Magee Mor Matthew* (9.820–21); but it is difficult to find as many male diminutives of this sort in Joyce as there are female diminutives, regardless of tradition—although they abound in Yeats and Synge. What is important to our reading of Joyce and his onomastic maneuvering is a sense of how he uses or misuses traditional naming practices.

Mary Seeman, who has worked on names and dreams, suggests that unconscious associations frequently emerge in nicknaming as they do in dreams. Explaining the psychological motives behind nicknaming, Seeman notes that "nicknames are derived from names in much the same way as dreams are derived from reality, by an unconscious transforming process that utilizes regression, duplication, displacement, condensation, reversal, and symbolization" ("Unconscious Meaning" 240–41). In his novel *Moon Palace* (1989), Paul Auster details his characters' fascination with names and nicknames, inscribing the often hilarious circumstances that lead to their understanding of both:

> Uncle Victor loved to concoct elaborate, nonsensical theories about things, and he never tired of expounding on the glories hidden in my name. Marco Stanley Fogg. According to him, it proved that travel was in my blood, that life would carry me to places where no man had ever been before. Marco, naturally enough, was for Marco Polo, the first European to visit China; Stanley was for the American journalist who had tracked down Dr. Livingstone "in the heart of darkest Africa"; and Fogg was for Phileas, the man who had stormed around the globe in less than three months. (6)

After a few weeks in a new Chicago school, Auster's young Fogg finds out that "names are the easiest thing to attack" (7), and is soon startled by his classmates' "spontaneous mutilations," butcherings that reveal the same psychological motivations Seeman discusses in her work on naming and dreams:

> The *o* at the end of Marco was obvious enough, yielding epithets such as Dumbo, Jerko, and Mumbo Jumbo, but what they did in other ways defied all expectations. Marco became Marco Polo; Marco Polo became Polo Shirt; Polo Shirt became Shirt Face; and Shirt Face became Shit Face—a dazzling bit of cruelty that stunned me the first time I heard it. (7)

Seeman explains that when we invent nicknames for others, we often proceed through gaps and leaps of logic, spontaneously connecting in our minds the person and her or his new name with the oddest assortment of things, many times going through a process much like the one outlined in Auster's novel—a process that surpasses logic and one that opts, instead, for pure, uncensored association. The processes that intervene during the renaming of Fogg are more readily understood after they are dismantled—just as we do with our dreams: in retrospect, after we trace the metamorphoses of certain elements, once we begin to recognize patterns and understand relationships between juxtaposed parts of a dream, we can identify the motivations and desires from which the dream generates.

Seeman's work can inform a variety of approaches to the *Wake*, since naming and dreaming are essential elements of Joyce's *Wake*, and since a number of readers contend that the book is Earwicker's dream of himself under the self-assumed name *Porter*, a pseudonym derived from his occupation as a bartender. Yet Seeman's research can also augment the study of women's names throughout Joyce's canon, particularly the infinite supply of nicknames or diminutives he assigned to his women characters, as exemplified by the following cursory list culled from *Dubliners, Ulysses*, and *Finnegans Wake: Nannie Flynn, Evvy Hill* (also called *Poppens* by Frank), *Ada Farrington, Polly Mooney, Annie Chandler, Lizzie Fleming, Kate Morkan, Molly Ivors*, and *Lily* the Caretaker's daughter; *Molly* and *Milly Bloom, Sally* and *Crissie Goulding, Lily Carlilse, Martha Mady Clifford* (who tells Bloom in Circe that her real name is *Peggy Griffin* [15.765–66], another diminutive), *Josie Breen, Susy Dignam, Boody, Maggy, Dilly,* and *Katey Dedalus, Gerty MacDowell, Cissy Caffrey, Edy Boardman, Floey, Atty,* and *Hetty Dillon, Mamy, Budgy,* and *Mina Purefoy, Mina Kennedy, Minnie Watchman, Bridie Kelly, Kitty, Fanny, Biddy the Clap,* and *Florry; Kate, Issy,* and *Vanessy*—these are just a handful of Joyce's women characters whose names have been transformed into diminutives or recast as nicknames. Of course, a number of men in Joyce's fiction have nicknames but their names are not characteristically diminutive; instead, the names have physiognomic connotations and associations that call attention to the male body, physical attributes, sexual prowess, or personality traits, as in the following examples: *Pisser Burke, Nosey Flynn, Thomas Squaretoes, Pimply Meissel, Hoppy Holohan, Bags Comisky, Mackerel, Buck Mulligan, Tusker Boyle, Blazes Boylan, Maggot O'Reilly, Foxy Campbell, Nasty Roche, Peter Pickackafax,* and *Kinch, the knifeblade*. Even the surnames *Athy* and *Cantwell* translate into puns that call attention to the male body. The men's names and nicknames often suggest action and sexual potency, and clearly differ from the diminutives of the women's names. Importantly, the male nicknames are often synecdochic—representing the total person by one of his properties, most often that which is most prized (or most feared) by the narrator/author himself.

The irony behind these sexually charged names is that at the time Joyce was writing *Dubliners* and *Ulysses,* and surely during the time periods in which each was set, a large percentage of Ireland's bachelors were still relatively celibate, as Mary Lowe-Evans suggests in *Crimes against Fecundity: Population Control in the Works of James Joyce:* "as a way of improving and maintaining one's standard of living, postponed marriages or celibacy was often chosen as an alternative to emigration" (9). Moreover, she adds, "after the Great Famine, the Irish began to take their economic plight more seriously than ever before and [began] to respond to it at every level of activity"—and sexuality was one of the levels of activity (9). In giving his male characters sexually charged nicknames, Joyce satirizes not only the traditional and expected link between naming and identity but the permanent celibacy adopted both by so many of his contemporaries decades after the Famine and by the priesthood. M'Coy's initial question, repeated by others throughout the novel *Ulysses,* "Who's getting it up?" (5.153), becomes all the more comical in Joyce's scheme of things, since we realize that very few of Joyce's male characters are—regardless of what their names might imply.

While Molly's name, like her mother's, is a source for feminist conjecture—we wonder who assigned it, for example—Molly's nominal memory is of interest, too, since for all her attention to names, it is often shabby. She cannot recall, for example, the first name of Lieutenant Mulvey, and although most readers assume it to be Harry, the text lacks any clearly definitive evidence. Molly thinks, "Molly darling he called me what was his name Jack Joe Harry Mulvey was it yes I think" (18.817–18), a trio that recalls Bloom's three guesses at the name of James Carey: "Like that Peter or Denis or James Carey that blew the gaff on the invincibles" (8.442–43). Since the name *Harry* is last in the trio of Molly's guessed names, it is easy to speculate about the lieutenant's full name, tempting, even, since her pattern of guessed names mimics Bloom's, where he gets the name right on the third try. But Molly cannot recall Mulvey's name, and she doesn't settle upon the name *Harry* but ends her guessing at that point, noting that with Mulvey names were always indeterminate, since he characteristically called everything a "whatyoucallit everything was whatyoucallit" (18.820). In fact, the designation "Jack Joe Harry Mulvey" is much like the traditional

"Tom, Dick, and Harry" signifier afforded the typical man in the street, not only because the trio of names ends in Harry, but because the *ck* in Jack and the medial *o* in Joe resemble letters in the names of the popularly cultivated threesome. Mulvey's name, however, remains indeterminate not only because Molly can't recall it but because some uncertainty effects all names in Joyce's works: a question mark hovers over a number of names in *Ulysses*, and Molly's rendering of Lieutenant Mulvey's name is no exception. After "nearly 20 years" (18.823), Molly can be forgiven any memory lapse but it is important to our understanding of Molly's unconscious that she forgets, misremembers, or is uncertain about the name of her first love. Her memory is unreliable, in other words, but as such, it helps to place Mulvey in the "big picture" of Molly's love life, suggesting that by June 1904, he is no longer as central a figure as Bloom.

Memory, in fact, plays an essential role in any author's manipulation of literary onomastics. Memory does a lot to names. In Bloom's misremembering of the name *Penrose,* for example, he thinks *Pendennis,* instead: "What was the name of that priestylooking chap was always squinting in when he passed? . . . Pen something. Pendennis? My memory is getting. Pen . . . ? Of course it's years ago" (8.176–79). In their introduction to *Who's He When He's at Home,* the Benstocks discuss Bloom's nominal error (16–17) and relate it to an earlier error of Bloom's when he substituted the name *Denis Carey* for *James Carey:* "That the name Denis persists in his mind as a bugaboo of sorts can be evidenced both from the substitution of Pendennis for Penrose, and earlier Denis Carey for James Carey" (17). It has not escaped Bernard Benstock's attention that the name *Pendennis* is a name surrounded in phallic suggestions—like the name *Penrose.* Indeed, the middle syllable of *Pendennis,* the *denn* that separates the two syllables of *Pen-is,* affords Bloom, the namemaker, a longer penis. Such orthographical extenders are not uncommon where Joycean penises are concerned. Just as an extra vowel in the name *Peeter the Picker* extends the length of Peter's member (Peeter's "peter," *FW* 616.09), the additional *n* in the word *pennis* (*FW* 495.23) suggests the same, especially since the "pennis" is in a "sluts maschine" (*FW* 495.23). Memory often distorts names, confusing them, and the reader can feel disoriented or bewildered among the nominal clutter. Brook Thomas plaintively asks, for example, "Do we have Pendennis or Penrose? Kendal Bushe or Seymour Bushe? Sidney Lee or Simon Lazarus? Purefoy or Beaufoy? Crofton or Crofter or Crawford?" (121). Much along the same lines, Bloom ponders in Sirens over his habitual error with the name *Figatner,* wondering, "Why do I always think Figather? Gathering figs, I think" (*U* 11.149–50). Bloom turns the name into a visual pun, a rebus, confusing his faulty mnemonic with the merchant's actual name. Memory, or a faulty memory, turns names into the impostures Stephen Dedalus warns us about in the Eumaeus chapter of *Ulysses.*

Sometimes the mnemonics are revealing, though, as when Bloom thinks of the name of the priest performing absolution at Dignam's funeral: "Father Coffey. I knew his name was like a coffin. Dominena-mine" (6.595). Here, the visual mnemonic is comically appropriate, since Father Coffey is performing the final phases of the funeral before Dignam's coffin is buried. A moment later Bloom muses on another name, *Peter* (6.597), when he recalls what Jesus said before he changed his disciple's name from *Simon* ("hearer"; Gifford *"Ulysses" Annotated* 118) to *Peter* ("rock"; Gifford 118): "Thou art Peter, and upon this rock I will build my church," an utterance that led Joyce to claim that the Catholic Church was founded upon a pun.

Freud, who argues that forgetting and misremembering proper names always serve an unconscious purpose, calls name jokes and onomastic puns "tendentious," suggesting in *Jokes and Their Relation to the Unconscious* that "jokes that play about with proper names often have an insulting and wounding purpose" (91). More often, it is the name's comical or ironic relation to a personality that amuses us, he explains. Interested in the name or names that one substitutes for a forgotten proper name, Freud argues in *The Psychopathology of Everyday Life* that "this displacement is not left to arbitrary psychical choice but follows paths which can be predicted and which conform to laws. In other words," Freud wrote in 1901, "I suspect that the name or names which are substituted are connected in a discoverable way with the missing name" (2) and are most likely motivated by repression (7). In Freudian light, the *"Denis* bugaboo" that persists in Bloom's mind may be an attempt at repressing his own sexuality or sexual vigor, since *Denis = Penis* with the protrusion lopped off.

While errors and memory lapses often lead in Joyce to serendipitous onomastic comedy, Joyce also inscribes the more serious politics of naming in his work, particularly as it affects gender. So far as women are concerned, every surname is a misrepresentation since it cata-logues women in terms of their fathers or husbands.[1] Throughout his canon, Joyce inscribes women's onomastic concerns by tying issues of women's naming to concepts of economics, politics, and physiognomy, linking concerns of wealth, gender, and gynecology in his practice of literary onomastics. This group of organizing principles governs the selection and assignment of names to his female characters.

Joyce initially links the issues of women's naming and economics through an allusion to Shakespeare's *Othello* where the villainous Iago compares one's good name to one's wealth. Shakespeare explains the name in monetary terms, and this is important to our understanding of women, naming, and patriarchy, since women in patriarchal cultures are economically disadvantaged because they are commodified and treated as objects to barter, often relying upon men for economic status. Shakespeare's Iago explains the importance of a name in economic terms, saying, "he that filches from me my good name / Robs me of that which not enriches him / And makes me poor indeed" (3.3.159–61). If a name is one's tie to riches, then imposing paternal or spousal names upon women is one more way to ensure their powerlessness and poverty. Joyce alludes to Iago's speech a number of times in his works. Vincent Cheng identifies it in the Dawn chapter of *Finnegans Wake:* "Respassers should be purseaccoutred. Qui stabat Meins quantum qui stabat Peins" (*FW* 594.14–15; Cheng 187, 225). Joyce briefly refers to Iago's speech in *Ulysses* when Lyster mocks Richard Best, who is reluctant to hear about Shakespeare's ill use of the name *Richard*, and complains, saying, "That is my name, Richard, don't you know. I hope you are going to say a good word for Richard, don't you know, for my sake. . . . I hope Edmund is going to catch it. I don't want Richard, my name....." (9.903–17). Best's complaint is drowned out by laughter, according to Joyce's stage directions, to which Lyster replies *a tempo*, "But he that filches from me my good name....." (9.919), a timely allusion appropriate in a chapter so filled with onomastic manipulations, not least among these his own, rendered in dramatic form as *QUAKER-LYSTER*. Of course, devaluing a name, stealing it, or, as Iago suggests, sullying it, is by all means a filching, and Iago's character makes these sentiments ironic, since he sets out in *Othello* to discredit Desdemona's name. Such injurious behavior is an act of thievery, and like any other act of thievery, it often necessitates a timely and appropriate revenge. Joyce authors Shakespeare's revenge when, in Circe, he renders Iago's name as "Iagogo" and "Iagogogo!" (15.3828–3829), substituting Iago's nominal mutilation with Joycean onomastic retaliation.

Not all sullied reputations effect retaliation, though. Lenehan is surprised, for example, when, after claiming to have seen Molly in deshabille, he gets no appropriate response from Bloom (14.1464–1502), no revenge against the soiling of Bloom's wife's, his "dona's," name (the *OED* defines *dona* as "a Spanish or Portuguese lady"); and the listeners are "Stunned like, seeing as how no shiners is acoming. Underconstumble?" (14.1499–1500). Though most readers associate "shiners" with coins, the word also suggests another shiner—a black eye—and the gossipers wonder whether Bloom has understood Lenehan's assertions or not, asking in their drunkenness, "Underconstumble?" (14.1500). It is probable that Bloom hears part of Lenehan's remarks, since the gossip is punctuated early on with the interrogation "Sir?" (14.1480), a word we can attribute to Bloom's characteristic *politesse*. In fact, in the first exchange Bloom has outside his home on the morning of 16 June, he "sirs" Mr. O'Rourke who, incidentally, does not sir him back until he meets him again in Circe (15.1673). It is likely, then, that Bloom's "Sir?" interrupts Lenehan's discussion, a discussion immediately steered toward the topic of "spud[s] again the rheumatiz" and the poppycock of such an old wives' tale (14.1480–1481):

> Know his dona? Yup, sartin I do. Full of a dure. See her in her dishybilly. Peels off a credit. Lovey lovekin. None of your lean kine, not much. Pull down the blind, love. . . . Got a prime pair of mincepies, no kid. . . . Must be seen to be believed. . . .
>   . . . Smutty Moll for a mattress jig. And a pull all together. *Ex!*
> (14.1474–1498)

What is interesting about this passage are the echoes it contains from the passage in Wandering Rocks where Lenehan tells M'Coy about the carriage ride he took with Bloom, Molly, and Chris Callinan after the dinner at the Glencree Reformatory. The reference to Molly is made clear through Joyce's repetition of terms like *mince pies, prime,* and *fine pair*—all words that characterize Molly's teeming sexuality:

> —But wait till I tell you, he said. Delahunt of Camden street had the catering and yours truly was chief bottlewasher. Bloom and the wife were there. Lashings of stuff we put up: port wine and sherry and curaçoa to which we did ample justice. Fast and furious it was. After liquids came solids. Cold joints galore and mince pies . . . .

—I know, M'Coy said. The year the missus was there .....
    Lenehan linked his arm warmly.
—But wait till I tell you, he said. . . . She [Molly] was well primed with a
good load of Delahunt's port under her bellyband. Every jolt the bloody
car gave I had her bumping up against me. Hell's delights! She has a fine
pair, God bless her. Like that.
    He held his caved hands a cubit from him, frowning. (10.545–61)

While it is decidedly difficult to establish which characters are doing
the talking toward the end of Oxen, linguistic clues such as these—
echoed references to mince pies, fine pairs, and the distinctive language of particular characters—act as markers that not only are neces-
sary to ascertain the plot of the novel but are helpful in allowing us to
figure out who the speaker is, and in turn, the unnamed target of his
encoded slander. In this case, Lenehan is speaking of Molly, referring
to her as "Smutty Moll" and claiming that he has slept with her, since
he seems to be repeating her own request that he "pull down the blind,
love," something Molly corroborates unwittingly when she recalls making love with Boylan: "I took off all my things with the blinds down"
(18.146).[2] In Penelope, Molly also recalls Lenehan's behavior the night
of the annual dinner, the night of the "boiled shirt affair" (10.537), and
thinks contemptuously of the irritating "sponger" who was "making
free with [her] after the Glencree dinner coming back that long joult
over the featherbed mountain" (18.427–28).

    It is not surprising that the name *Moll* itself would suggest to
Lenehan and company a prostitute or lady of the evening—hence, the
"Smutty Moll" reference, since the word *moll* is slang for a prostitute.
Molly is referred to earlier in the chapter as *"Mrs Moll"* (14.509) when
the narrator briefly recounts Bloom's dream of her in red slippers and
Turkish trunks. An unusual form of her name, and one that strengthens her onomastic association with Lenehan's *"Smutty Moll,"* the *"Mrs
Moll"* reference corroborates Lenehan's account of Molly. Moreover,
the name recalls the earlier *"Mrs Marion Bloom,"* a form of address that
annoys Bloom in Calypso when he retrieves a letter addressed to her
that way, since it circumvents her marital name, *"Mrs Leopold Bloom."*

    Further, Lenehan's suggestion of a "mattress jig" with Molly is not
surprising, either: although he uses *jig* in the sense of the dance, the
word is associated with Molly's mattress and its noisy quoits, which
appear in Circe jingling and jigjagging (15.1136–1138). Interestingly,
Lenehan describes Molly's breasts as mince pies in a way that echoes

Bloom's earlier sexual metaphor, "Prime sausage" (4.179), when at the butcher shop he thinks of the size of an imaginary policeman's penis. Molly's breasts generate another name for her, "*Marion of the bountiful bosoms*" (12.1007) when she is described by one of the Cyclops narrators as "Pride of Calpe's rocky mount, the ravenhaired daughter of Tweedy" (12.1003). But apart from the physical evidence that might make Lenehan's remarks credible—Molly is referred to as "a buxom lassy" (11.502), for example—Molly corroborates Lenehan's statement by using the word *smutty* herself in Calypso and Penelope. When Bloom asks whether she finished *Ruby: The Pride of the Ring*, she replies, "Yes. . . . There's nothing smutty in it" (4.354), but then goes on to question Bloom about the outcome of the book: "Is she in love with the first fellow all the time?" (4.355–56). Molly's plot-specific question indicates that she stopped reading *Ruby* because it lacked nasty bits, because there was "nothing smutty in it." *Smutty* also occurs at the beginning of Penelope (18.22) and at the end of Penelope, where Molly suggests that she'll "let out a few smutty words" to drive Bloom mad (18.1531). Framing the narrative of the chapter much as the word *yes* does, *smutty* is a word associated with Molly's discourse. It is not unlikely, then, that the name "Smutty Moll" refers to her, and this is important because it indicates not only the kind of gossip about Molly that was bandied about Dublin that afternoon but also the male perception of her. Though Molly is given only eight names throughout *Ulysses*,[3] the names associate her either with illicit behavior of one kind or another or with saintliness, as in the name *S. Marion Calpensis* (12.1710), a name that connects her with Calpe (Gibraltar). Molly's names, unlike Bloom's and Stephen's, are all given to her by others; she does not name herself at all. With the exception of the names Molly's mother gives her, all of the names Molly receives are given to her by men, and they reflect the social/sexual biases of the early 1900s. Molly is stereotyped as the conventional virgin/whore, and the Dublin males see her in ways that are predictably determined by Victorian culture and tradition.

Molly's reputation around Dublin is colored not only by her sensual appearance but by her stage career as well. Mr. Power, smiling, refers to Molly as *madame* in Hades (6.224), and later, in the same chapter, Ned Lambert refers to her by her stage name, *Madame Marion Tweedy*, assuring John Henry Menton that she's got plenty of game left in her still (6.693, 6.706). A customary stage name for married women, *ma-*

dame was often used in turn-of-the-century Victorian Dublin, and Molly used it herself even before she married Bloom. The *OED* explains that the term *madame* was assumed by British and American singers or musicians, and by other professional women engaged in businesses such as dressmaking where native taste or skill is reputed to be inferior. Molly's use of the appellation *Madame*, then, is probably meant to signal her operatic expertise and her experience as a European performer. Another example of its use occurs in the name *Madame Glynn*, the singer "imported" from London to perform in Holohan's concert in the short story "A Mother."[4] As it is applied to Molly, the *Madame* appellation is interesting because although it connotes *Mrs.*, it is used not before Molly's married name, as is customary, but before her maiden name: *Madame Marion Tweedy*.

Given the Shakespearean equation of a name and money, however, it is interesting that most of Molly's names are generated on account of her stage career. Importantly, Molly selects her "own" name when any sort of business transaction is involved. She performs on stage under the name *Marion Tweedy*, for example, and likewise, although the name *"Mrs Marion Bloom"* annoys Leopold when he reads it on the envelope of Boylan's letter (4.243–45)—"Bold hand. Mrs Marion," he thinks to himself (4.244, 4.311), put off by Boylan's circumvention of Molly's formal marital name—*"Mrs Marion Bloom"* may be a name Molly prefers for herself, since it is the way she chooses to write her name in the newspaper advertisement about her sale of clothing, an advertisement that Simon Dedalus recalls with wry humor in Sirens: "Mrs Marion Bloom has left off clothes of all descriptions" (11.496–97). Boylan does not use Molly's professional name on the day's correspondence, though the missive is ostensibly a professional one. Moreover, Molly chastises Bloom in Circe for not allowing her the *Mrs. Marion* name, saying, "Mrs Marion from this out, my dear man, when you speak to me" (15.306), and although he heeds her scolding immediately thereafter when he meets up with Sweny and discusses the special recipe body lotion for his wife, "Mrs Marion" (15.345), he ignores Molly's request throughout the remainder of the chapter. While it seems that Bloom at one time suggested that Molly use the name *"Mrs Marion Bloom"* in a lost-and-found ad in the *Irish Times* to reclaim the suede gloves she left in the women's room at the Dublin Bakery the day she first met Boylan (18.256), Bloom denies Molly the independent name *Marion* when he asserts in Circe that her name is *"Lady Bloom"*

(15.1677), thrusting his own identity upon her and defining her in terms of his own name. To be sure, Bloom's nominal suggestion for the advertisement was most likely part of his "pimping" scheme; that is, Joyce suggests that Bloom choreographed Molly and Boylan's encounter, assuming that the introduction would lead to an adulterous affair. If this is correct, then it is no surprise that Bloom would sanction Molly's use of "*Mrs Marion Bloom*" in an advertisement that would probably catch Boylan's eye. In effect, Bloom's unwillingness to yield to Molly's "Mrs Marion" name can be read not only in economic terms, since the *Marion* rubric seems to designate her "other" life—her stage life, her professional life, indeed, her life with Boylan—but in Shakespearean terms, as well, since it is an attempt to erase or "filch" the wife's name.

Names are often tied to economics. Mrs. Kearney of "A Mother" knows that; in fact, she realizes that even typography is an economic issue: "As Mr Holohan was a novice in such delicate matters as the wording of bills and the disposing of items for a programme Mrs Kearney helped him. She had tact. She knew what *artistes* should go into capitals and what *artistes* should go into small type" (D 138). "A Mother" is a story about names and economics. In the second sentence of the story, the reader learns that Mr. Holohan's nickname is Hoppy and shortly thereafter that "Miss Devlin had become Mrs Kearney out of spite" (D 136).[5] In fact, it is only when Mrs. Kearney determines to "take advantage of her daughter's name" (137) that the trouble begins. Further, O'Madden Burke, a latecomer to the concert series and surrogate columnist who will write up the notice for the *Freeman*, is outspokenly critical of the Kearney women. Burke, however, is also important because of his own name: "His magniloquent western name was the moral umbrella upon which he balanced the fine problem of his finances. He was widely respected" (145). The story closes as O'Madden Burke is "poised upon his umbrella in approval" (149). Burke's name is his umbrella, a protective, impenetrable, and impervious sheath, much like the nominal drapery introduced in the early *Dubliners* stories.

Importantly, the Kearney women are not protected by their names—in fact, it is precisely Kathleen's name that makes her vulnerable. Joyce, no doubt, carefully selected the name *Holohan*, like the name *Kathleen*, for inclusion in this story—a point I argue in chapter 1—since the name echoes the surname of Kathleen ni Houlihan, the personification of

Ireland and subject of the 1902 play by W. B. Yeats, *Cathleen ni Houlihan*,[6] which focuses on issues of economics and politics. In the *Dubliners* story, then, naming and economics are intertwined and both play a major role. Another interesting name in "A Mother" is *Healy*, the name assigned to the young woman and friend of the Kearneys, who, in the last moments of the story, turns on the young pianist and agrees to accompany the concert performers in Kathleen's absence. Miss Healy's timely "betrayal" dashes the magnificence of Mrs. Kearney's audacious last stand, and we might imagine the Kearney women uttering under their breath as they exit the concert hall, "Et tu, Healy?"—an implied reference that alludes not only to Joyce's first published piece of writing, but to the Brutus-like betrayal of Parnell. Just as the names *Kathleen* and *Holohan* extend the allusiveness of each other, the name *Healy* highlights and politicizes the betrayal in the story.

Economics is often, if not always, tied to issues of politics, as Joyce's work demonstrates. But the politics of naming are not those of church, country, or state; rather, Joyce associates women's names with the politics of gender. According to the myths of creation, Adam named everything in the universe except for his wife, whom he allowed to name herself. Although Milton does not broach the subject of how Eve was named, Eve's self-naming merits our investigation specifically because a number of Joyce's women characters act out a sort of Eve Syndrome, displaying both a characteristic and typical desire to name themselves.

It is interesting that Eve chose for herself the palindromic name *Hawwah*, a word that means "life" in Hebrew. A nominal figure that reads the same backward or forward, the palindrome is also known as *versus diabolici*, since the Devil is said to have concocted it; its diabolical character seems to lie in its circularity, denying the irreversibility of time. There is something mystical about a palindrome in that it inhibits interruption, it warns against violation, it refuses decoding. It is a puzzle that cannot be mastered or deciphered. Consequently, a number of women's names in Joyce are seemingly palindromic—ALP's first name *Anna* (or as she is also called in the *Wake, Nan*), *Ada Farrington*, and even the names *Emma* and *Issy* seem to do the same sort of thing. While all four are not precise palindromes, the names turn back on themselves, announcing their circularity. The names *Emma* and *Issy* are what we might call phonetic palindromes, since the syllables of the names echo each other backward: "Emma"; "Issy." With Issy, the reversal effect is further reinforced by her association with mirrors. Likewise, the way that Joyce arranges and rearranges the initials *A. L. P.* throughout the *Wake* suggests the figure of the palindrome because of the way the initials tumble over one another, asserting in their continual rearrangement a circularity and infinity associated with Eve's palindrome. Though HCE's letters tumble and persistently regroup, his initials do not have similar properties; that is, while ALP's letters fall into configurations that form recognizable English words—*pal, alp, lap*—or arrange themselves into familiar phonetic patterns—such as *pla* [play], or *apl* [apple—Eve?]—HCE's name, his letters, do not have the same sort of suggestiveness on their own, nor do they form recognizable words. The palindromic tumbling particularly suits the women's names, signaling their alignment with Eve, an empowered namer.

The impulse toward self-naming is not an unusual one for female characters in a modernist text. The heroine of Jean Rhys's *Good Morning, Midnight*, for example, explains her name change early in the text:

> Was it in 1923 or 1924 that we lived round the corner, in the Rue Victor-Cousin, and Enno bought me that Cossack cap and the imitation astrakhan coat? It was then that I started calling myself Sasha. I thought it might change my luck if I changed my name. Did it bring me any luck, I wonder—calling myself Sasha? (12)

After the name change, Sasha Jensen resents those who refuse to honor her new name and thinks, "It's so like him . . . that he refuses to call me Sasha, or even Sophie. No, it's Sophia, full and grand" (42). Naming, certainly to Sasha, and to Joyce's women characters, is political; it is either done *by* patriarchy, or in defiance *of* patriarchy. We do not know, for example, why Anna Livia Plurabelle's surname is different from Earwicker's, but the name surely suggests her independence as woman, as river, as goddess and Eve figure, and her transcendence of patriarchal confines. When the name occurs in its sole undistorted form in the *Wake*, it announces its transcendence of the confines of temporality as well: "Anna was, Livia is, Plurabelle's to be" (*FW* 215.24). The name *Plurabelle* suggests that Anna Livia is many women, just as she is many rivers. In fact, because her surname differs from Earwicker's, the washerwomen question the circumstances of ALP's marriage to HCE, asking, "How elster is he a called at all? Qu'appelle? Huges Caput Earlyfouler" (197.7–8). They also question the matrimonial details, suggesting that the couple's marriage banns were never announced or that the service was performed by a captain: "Was her banns never loosened in Adam and Eve's or were him and her but captain spliced?" (197.11–13). ALP's name makes her the subject of discourse—because of her name, she is transmutated into a suspicious figure.

Musing upon her given and self-adopted names is often symptomatic of the female heroine, and the tensions that result from her adherence to or rejection of patriarchal onomastics often provide a violent subtext to the novels, short stories, or poems that contain the heroine. By naming herself, the woman asserts a self-defined personality, a personality she decrees to be her own. Women's autonomastics, then, announces a calculated rejection of male definitions, while at the same time it heralds woman's reevaluation of the self. Signaling a clear break from the patriarchal constructs of naming, autonomastics provides women with eternal incognitos, weaponry against the stratagems of male definition. When women take their own names, when women disjoin themselves from the system of male naming, they no longer have to involve themselves in the patriarchal world described by Matthew O'Connor in *Nightwood* as one of "rape, murder and all abominations" (88).[7] Autonomastics is for women an easily accessible mode of expatriation in that it allows women a thumbprint, an identity, set against nowhere in the world, and it challenges their own ineffectuality when aligned with the politics of naming. Such politics abound in Joyce's canon, where Joyce's women struggle against the confines of their names.

Specifically, how do women in Joyce's works reveal their struggles? How do they mark their positions? Eveline Hill, the protagonist of the *Dubliners* story "Eveline," for example, successfully extricates herself from the confines of her "Eve" name since, like her nameling in the Garden of Eden who was tempted by promises of knowledge, Eveline, too, is tempted: "He had tales of distant countries. . . . He told her the names of the ships he had been on and the names of the different services. He had sailed through the Straits of Magellan and he told her stories of the terrible Patagonians" (*D* 39).[8] Apparently, Eveline is seduced by names—names of ships, names of "different services," and personal names—Frank's, her own, and her brother's, as well. A brief look at two of the men's names in this story is revealing: it is interesting that Eveline's favorite brother is named *Ernest*, a name that suggests a sincere and purposeful person, while her lover's name, *Frank*, bears equally attractive associations, since it connotes a candid, open, and straight-from-the-shoulder man. And Eveline describes him as such, thinking, "Frank was very kind, manly, open-hearted" (*D* 38). Hugh Kenner briefly notes that "Frank is the right name for a man like that; there would have been no story if he had told [Eveline] that his name was Boris" ("Molly's Masterstroke" 20). Traditionally, though, it is more common for women to be given "virtue names" like those of the two men in the story, *Ernest* and *Frank*; and while Joyce is faithful to verisimilitude in nearly every aspect of his art—including his literary onomastics—here he tampers with traditional naming patterns by assigning virtue names to male characters, and by assigning the name *Frank* ironically to a character whom Kenner describes as nothing short of "a bounder with a glib line, who tried to pick himself up a piece of skirt" (21). Recent critical attention has focused on the character of Frank[9]—but Eveline is not to be supplanted by her male counterpart in the story.

Eveline's dilemma is that she does not want to be treated as her mother was. Angered by Miss Gavan's contemptuous treatment of her, Eveline theorizes, "In her new home, in a distant unknown country, it would not be like that. Then she would be married—she, Eveline. People would treat her with respect then. She would not be treated as her mother had been" (*D* 37). This passage shows the contradictions in Eveline's mind: she thinks that being married will guarantee respect; yet the example of her mother should tell her otherwise. To be sure, unmarried women in *Dubliners* do not generate a great deal of respect; this is made clear in the way that Maria is treated in "Clay," where she is humored by the "evidently annoyed" shop girl who asks Maria "was it wedding-cake she wanted to buy" (102);[10] made the butt of a joke by the next-door girls who put clay on one of the saucers; and patronized by Joe, Mrs. Donnelly, and the rest of her audience who, out of pity, do not point out the error in her singing. Eveline does not want to be treated "as her mother had been," but she refuses, nonetheless, to elope with Frank. Though Eveline returns to her "life of commonplace sacrifices" and is doomed to celibacy, no doubt, Eveline's choice to remain in Dublin is informed by her past; she does not want to be treated as her mother had been yet she stays in Dublin to become her mother, catering to her father and to "the two young children who had been left to her charge" (38). It is important to realize that Eveline's escape is thwarted not by fear, not by naivete, but by her sense of responsibility. Just as Blessed Margaret Mary Alacoque—the saint whose picture hangs on the wall in the Hill home (37)—was cured of a self-inflicted paralysis when she vowed to consecrate herself to a holy life (Dolch 100), and give herself to the literally "open hearted" [*frank*] Jesus, Eveline, too, is arguably freed when she chooses to return to the life she knows, though like an ironized Margaret Mary, she is afraid to embrace the sacred heart.[11] The sacrifice, however, frees her. Perhaps this is too "Catholic" a reading of "Eveline," but the very title of the story, like the name of the main character, presupposes and invites a religious interpretation.

Eveline, so named, brings Garden of Eden politics crashing into Dublin's playground, a notion Joyce himself entertains in *Finnegans Wake* where the "Eve and Adam" reference (3.1) identifies prelapsarian Dublin. Having tied policies of naming to issues of economics, politics, and gender, Joyce takes his literary onomastics one step further and inscribes in some women's names a kind of circularity that mimics the woman's body. John Paul Riquelme works in his 1983 *Teller and Tale in Joyce's Fiction* with Joyce's *Finnegans Wake* narratives and the Moebius strip, the puzzling, geometric one-sided novelty. As a controlling metaphor, the Moebius strip works well to describe the many encircling stories, the multiple mosaics, that make up the *Wake*. But the metaphor of the Moebius strip can be extended beyond the narrative, apart from concerns of theme, narrative, structure, and form. The Moebius strip works equally well with units of language, within the language itself, on a smaller scale, to focus specifically on names in Joyce. Like a woman's body, both the paper configuration and the nominal configuration curve and fold upon itself, encircling its subject. A name, because it is both linear and round, is much like the "square circle" configuration Joyce used in his descriptions of the *Wake*. In fact, Joyce's own name mimics the Moebius strip in that its initials, *J. A. A. J.* (*James Augustine Aloysius Joyce*), are symmetrical, palindromic, and self-contained—like the snake that swallows its own tail. Of course, there is a tendency in Joyce to set up a pattern only to destroy it later, so few models and paradigms of naming apply to Joyce's entire work; but the Viconian concept of circularity and infinity seems applicable to many of Joyce's women's names.

In their introduction to *Women in Joyce*, Elaine Unkeless and Suzette Henke discuss two conflicting views of Joyce and women, noting that while Carl Jung praised Joyce for his "remarkable insight into the female psyche" (xi), Nora Joyce protested that her husband knew "nothing at all about women" (xi). Just as the women of *Dubliners* are "almost always portrayed in relation to men—as mothers, wives, daughters, sisters, lovers, or would-be spouses" (*Women in Joyce* xvi), they are also named in relation to men. Naming conventions, like the rest of language, have been shaped to meet the interests of society, and in patriarchal societies the shapers have been men (Miller and Swift 7). In Joyce's works, few women are drawn in the act of naming with the exceptions of women like Miss Kennedy, who refers to the old fogey at Boyd's as "*greasy eyes*" (*U* 11.169), a name responsible for the later rendering of Bloom as "*greaseabloom*" (11.180, 11.185); and Milly, who may have given Bloom the name *Papli* (4.397) since it sounds like a child's approximation of *Papa, Leopold,* or *Poldy,* much like the name "*Dante*" *Riordan* in *A Portrait* approximates the word *Aunty.* That so few women are namers in Joyce is important to our understanding of women and names since it may indicate Joyce's fidelity to the male system of naming, and to an aesthetic of verisimilitude. Naming is most obviously tied to issues of paternity, as we shall see in the next chapter; but it is also tied to issues of authority and apprehension, and that is why Joyce's onomastic *inventio* as it applies to his women characters is an important part of his rhetoric of nomenclature. In his works, women's names reveal a position of undecidability in that they both confine and liberate the women, defining them in terms of husbands and fathers, mothers, saints and whores, belittling them through diminutives, condemning them to indeterminacy (as in the name E—— C——), but steering them toward autonomastics, and endowing them, however briefly, with the power to name themselves. His female characters are privileged to rename themselves, to fashion their own names, names that indicate difference *from* rather than commonality *among*, enabling them to emerge from the veil of male onomastic drapery.

CHAPTER FOUR

Naming, Nameplay, and Revenge

Nameplay has its roots in Irish satirical tradition, the early Irish satirists having been feared for their maleficent verses, their mockery, and their magically injurious incantations. In Edmund Spenser's *Vewe of the Present State of Irelande* (1596), he notes that "theare is amongst the Irishe a certen kind of people Called Bardes . . ." (124). Spenser's description of the Irish bards is particularly important to our understanding of naming, nameplay, and revenge, since Spenser describes the bards' duties as being "in steade of Poets whose profession is to sett fourthe the praises and dispraises of menne in their Poems or Rymes" (124). Spenser censures the Irish bards because they "seldome use to Chose out themselves the doinges of good men for the arguments of theire poems but whom soever they finde to be most Licentious of life and desperate in all partes of disobedience and rebellious disposicion" (125). He probably did not understand the office of the Irish satirist, a figure whose rhymes often struck fear into the hearts of his listeners, a figure empowered by his penchant for cursing and blaming. In the Scylla and Charybdis chapter of *Ulysses*, Stephen appropriates this office, exercising in his nameplay a linguistic and intellectual revenge that is aimed at an unsuspecting audience.

James Snead discussed the link between nameplay and revenge particularly as it is practiced by Stephen in the library episode of *Ulysses* in his prefatory remarks in a session on character and contemporary theory at the 1984 James Joyce Symposium in Frankfurt:

> By "Scylla and Charybdis" Stephen has conceived how names can be detached from their owners. They are, therefore, infinitely manipulable—indeed, he perverts the names of his enemies in the National Library scene, trying out a form of rhetorical revenge against hitherto unassailable authorities. "Mr Secondbest Best," "beautifulinsadness Best," and

95

"ugling Eglinton," far from cute puns, may exemplify a form of linguistic deformation not unpolitical in nature. (145)

What I would like to examine in this chapter are the nominal manipulations that Stephen creates in Scylla and Charybdis. Stephen's naming in that episode is informed by his knowledge of Shakespeare's biography and canon, as in the name *Mr Secondbest Best* (*U* 9.714–15); by Stephen's own ideas about literature and language, as in the name *John Eclecticon* (9.1070); and by Stephen's ideas about history and about women, as in the name *Nell Gwynn Herpyllis* (9.723–24). Therefore, Scylla and Charybdis is a good episode in which to test the theories of naming outlined in the first three chapters of this book, since Stephen's naming incorporates elements of literary allusion, history, and patriarchy. An examination of Stephen's onomastics and the nature of influence, this chapter builds upon authorial and textual manipulations, paying particular attention to the nominal variations introduced by Stephen in a gesture of revenge or mutiny against figures more powerful than he, not least Shakespeare, construed as a dominant voice of English (not Irish) culture.

Rejecting a name, disallowing it, ignoring it, truncating it, replacing it, misspelling it, misprinting it, mispronouncing it, withholding it, disregarding conventionalized forms of it, devaluing it, or refusing to acknowledge particular parts of it (i.e., categorically omitting the personal name or surname)—these are acts that constitute nominal sedition, and, as we shall see, they are full of political import.

Ulysses, as well as Joyce's earlier and later works, contains dozens of instances where nameplay is used for retribution. Onomastic manipulation is an accessible and, more important, economic form of revenge for many of Joyce's characters who rename others not only in contempt but often in a gesture of humorous bravado, to display no want of wit. They often name others with allusive names, by appending to Bloom and to Stephen such names as *Ikey Moses* (9.607), *Ahasuerus* (12.1667), *Junius* (12.1633), *Tommy Tittlemouse* (15.1984–85), and *Macduff* (7.898); by appending to Bloom and to Stephen such nicknames as *Mackerel* (8.405), *Kinch* (1.08), and *Stephaneforos* (14.1121); and by appending to Haines, Stephen, Mulligan, Bloom, and Kernan, such descriptors as *Sassenach* (1.232), *bullockbefriending bard* (2.431), *Sonmulligan* (9.875), *Old lardyface* (12.1476–77), and *Tomgin Kernan* (11.1148). Nameplay is part of an Irish tradition, a tradition that is grounded in verbal and linguistic one-upmanship.

The disfiguring of names is a serious business, though it is often very comical in Joyce's work and in other places where the Irish penchant for theatricality manifests and amuses itself; yet it is traditionally an office reserved for the Irish bard who was both feared and admired for his ability to "nail a name" on a friend or foe. Terrence Des Pres explains the historical link between naming, satire, and bardic disfigurement in a discussion of Yeats and the ancient, bardic rat-rhymers, suggesting that "the blemish of a nickname" was one of the Gaelic bards' best defenses against an enemy:

> As late as the seventeenth century a famous bard (Teig, son of Daire) challenged his own patrons (the O'Briens) by threatening to "nail a name" on them with his "blister-raising ranns". . . . To "nail a name on a man" could ruin his tribal standing, destroy his reputation and the honor on which his personal worth depended. (42)

Des Pres explains that "mockery, invective and magical injury" were often involved in cursing of this sort (42), and that the potency or believed potency of the relevant rhymes, verses, and incantations endowed the rat-rhymers with a certain fame: "Irish bards were often more famous for their cursing than for their more constructive powers, their duties and privileges as ministers to the tribe" (38). In fact, the magical-religious functions of the cursers and rhymers went unquestioned until Patrick began the Christianization of Ireland in 432, Des Pres explains (39). Yeats was familiar with the rat-rhyming tradition and characteristically rat-rhymed his Abbey Theatre patrons in his poems, Des Pres argues—an ancient brand of retaliation, bardic blaming of this sort was usually aimed at unworthy patrons. Like Yeats, Joyce was surely familiar with the ancient cursing tactics. In a gesture of bardic alignment, Stephen attacks his conspicuously meager library audience in the Scylla and Charybdis episode of *Ulysses,* a coterie of the self-proclaimed Dublin literari, by disfiguring and manipulating their surnames, by "nailing names" on them.

Joyce himself often used naming as revenge—not to protect the innocent but to implicate the guilty, as Richard Ellmann reports (363–64). He also used naming to recall characters from earlier works, adding to the continuity of his canon. One such example occurs in the Nestor episode where Stephen's I.O.U. list contains names not only from the present novel but from real life and from Joyce's earlier writings, since Stephen's list of creditors in *Ulysses* includes characters from *A Portrait* and *Stephen Hero*. In response to Deasy's question, "*I paid my way. I never borrowed a shilling in my life.* Can you feel that? *I owe nothing.* Can you?," Stephen silently calculates an answer:

> Mulligan, nine pounds, three pairs of socks, one pair brogues, ties. Curran, ten guineas. McCann, one guinea. Fred Ryan, two shillings. Temple, two lunches. Russell, one guinea, Cousins, ten shillings, Bob Reynolds, half a guinea, Koehler, three guineas, Mrs MacKernan, five weeks' board. The lump I have is useless. (2.255–59)

Stephen is reminded of Fred Ryan in Scylla and Charybdis, when Russell tells Stephen that Ryan wants ample space in *Dana* to publish an essay on economics. Stephen muses over the monetary coincidence, thinking, "Fraidrine. Two pieces of silver he lent me. Tide you over. Economics" (9.1084). Just as economics and literary patronage informed the curses of the bardic rat-rhymers, Stephen practices a similar form of revenge in this passage, since the spontaneous onomastic assault contained in the name *Fraidrine* is leveled at both Ryan and Russell, who has just told Stephen that he "is the only contributor to *Dana* who asks for pieces of silver" (9.1081), the Judas connection being an obvious one. To be sure, many of the names in Scylla and Charybdis "suffer from rough handling by the narrative voice" (Benstocks *Who's He* 20), but most of the manipulated names in the chapter are names influenced by, if not issued from or determined by, Stephen Dedalus, since the episode, like Proteus, most closely approximates Stephen's thought and temperament, approaching his mind "almost as if he were himself the author of the narrator's words" (Bowen 474). The constant interplay between Stephen's cerebral manipulations of names and the narrating intelligence's nominal tomfoolery in the chapter, as well as Mulligan's periodic interruptions, makes it difficult to attribute the nominal play to either of the characters with any certainty. David Hayman argues that it is the "arranger" who is responsible for most of the narrative nameplay in the episode but I disagree. I suggest that Stephen generates most of the names in a gesture of mutiny and revenge to lash out privately at his "brood of mockers" (9.492).[1]

Stephen's revenge takes many forms. Culturally, naming is most closely associated with paternity, a theme that looms over the Scylla and Charybdis episode where Stephen tries to bastardize his small library audience by distorting their patronyms. Thus, *Lyster* becomes *Quakerlyster* (9.918); *Eglinton* becomes *Chin Chon Eg Lin Ton* and *Mageeglinjohn* (9.1129, 9.900); *Fred Ryan* becomes *Fraidrine* (9.1084); and *Best* and *Eglinton* become *Besteglinton* (9.728), a somewhat homosexual joining perhaps because of Best's effeminacy, which causes Stephen to link him with Wilde—"His glance touched their faces lightly as he smiled, a blond ephebe. Tame essence of Wilde" (9.531–32)—or possibly because Eglinton is a (presumably chaste) bachelor. The name *Eglinton* also suggests an eglantine or rose, a symbol associated with the vagina, and Stephen notes the phonetic and orthographic similarities between Eglinton and eglantine when he thinks, "Eglintoneyes, quick with pleasure, looked up shybrightly. Gladly glancing, a merry puritan, through the twisted eglantine" (9.872–73), a paragraph that both begins and ends with references to Eglinton's name. Importantly, all of these associations conspire against Eglinton in Stephen's naming process. The men's "new" names deform their surnames, and some of the names even emasculate the men, as in the names *Monk Mulligan* (9.773), *Cuck Mulligan* (9.1025), and *littlejohn* (9.367), names that imply celibacy, cuckoldry, and inadequate penis size, since *john* was a recognized slang term for the penis and condom from the late nineteenth to mid-twentieth century (Partridge 624–25). What Stephen tries to do to his audience this hour on 16 June 1904 is rid them of their fathers, and he does this first by breaking down their surnames, and by consequently emasculating them so that they cannot increase their family lines. Through retributive nameplay, Stephen halts regeneration, ending the possibility of fatherhood altogether, an institution that Stephen argues "may be a legal fiction" anyway (9.844).

Paternity is one of the guiding issues in this episode, not only so far as names are concerned, but so far as literary creation is concerned, as well. Joyce once said in appropriately heretical fashion that the act of creation was the *real* original sin, so he unites the acts of sin, creation, and the fury that fuels them in his writings. Maud Ellmann suggests that Joyce weaves "the naming and creation of the universe with the fury of the father and the son" (74), arguing that in Joyce as in Homer, naming and creation are intrinsic in fueling the father/son antagonism. In Scylla and Charybdis, Stephen's revenge against the father is an onomastic one: he wreaks his vengeance by manipulating the orthography and typography of names, including his own, and exploits the fortuitous associations they carry. By the time he and Mulligan leave the National Library, Stephen has accomplished what he set out to do: he has successfully bastardized his audience and himself. It is not a killing off of the father that Stephen executes in the library; rather, he displaces the father as the creative figure and Adamic namer. Patrick McGee notes that the emphasis throughout this chapter remains focused on Shakespeare's filial name, *Will*—his "signature among the stars"—rather than on his patronymic, and he adds that the recurrence of the name *Will* in the plays successfully designates Shakespeare without reference to his father (39–41; 65).

After Stephen works his theory, like Shakespeare, he becomes both father and son. As Zack Bowen describes the paradox in literary and procreative terms, "the artist's creation is both himself and his potential" (478). Yet Stephen's theory equates him not only with the eternal father/creator who, in the Trinity, is both father and son but with William Shakespeare and his son Hamnet—not merely because of the circumstances surrounding the production of *Hamlet*, either: the alignment is a genealogical one, too, since Hamnet Shakespeare, the son who died at age eleven in 1596, was christened with his twin sister, Judith, on Joyce's birthday, 2 February, in 1585.[2] No doubt, with all the superstitions Joyce had about his birthday (R. Ellmann 23, 451, 523, 569, 645, 715; B. Benstock 1–7), such a coincidence, if Joyce knew of it, would not go unnoticed. The coincidence of date, then, makes Joyce (as well as Stephen, who shares the same birthday) not only William Shakespeare but Shakespeare's son as well. Stephen's theory allows him not only to become Shakespeare, but to outdo him by becoming father and son, thereby taking Shakespeare's own theatrical stunt and going it one better. Vincent Cheng reports that Joyce was in the "lifelong habit" of "comparing himself with England's national poet" (1), and he cites Nora Joyce's comment to Frank Budgen, "Ah, there's only one man he's got to get the better of now, and that's that Shakespeare" (1). Buck Mulligan's amusing comment, "Shakespeare? . . . I seem to know the name" (*U* 9.508), condemns Shakespeare to near anonymity; but when he later refers to Stephen as "the bard Kinch" (9.1088), the descriptor is one that helps Stephen supplant Shakespeare—not only as father and progeniture but as author and creator. One might argue that Joyce succeeds in surpassing Shakespeare, that he becomes him, in fact, outwitting Shakespeare, death, *and* consubstantiality in the process.

Aside from his desire to align himself with his rival Shakespeare, why would Stephen's theory be so distinctly elaborate? James Michels suggests that Stephen's revenge is a murderous one, and that through his lengthy and convoluted theory, he slays his audience:

> Drawing upon a few thin parallels between the lives of Shakespeare and the librarians (*e.g.*, all claim to be artists, all claim an artistic ascendancy), Stephen creates his painful ironic contrasts between them. If he succeeds in making the *nature* of Shakespeare's life a necessary precondition of art, his hearers must see that they have failed as human beings and as artists. . . . Stephen intends his "mixture of theolologico-philolological," like the witches' brew in *Macbeth*, to be lethal indeed. (189–90)

Stephen's theory, interspersed as it is with nominal truncations and onomastic deviations, is more than a playful attempt to do away with his fidgety audience: a skeptical Eglinton, an in-and-out Lyster, an interrupting AE, and an effeminate Best. Rather, his nameplay rewards him with literary and rhetorical superiority, since it is a display of penetrating wit, well-turned allusion, and onomastic repartee. Importantly, all of the nameplay occurs in Stephen's mind, and this allows him not only creative privacy but an exercise of silence and cunning. The nominal manipulations do not alienate his audience—indeed, Stephen tries very hard to maintain friendliness even amid a sea of skepticism. He makes a point of flattering Eglinton, for example, when he repeats a point he had made earlier, saying, "for nature, as Mr Magee understands her, abhors perfection. . . . Flatter. Rarely. But flatter" (9.870–74). In order to keep his audience, Stephen must compliment them outwardly. Because Stephen is not by nature a sycophant, he retaliates against his own displays of kindness and flattery by wielding an interior penury that takes its form in nominal revenge.

Onomastic deformation is, for Stephen, a game, an intellectual exercise. Frederick Burelbach points out in an essay on the comedy of naming that Joyce often calls our attention to the "basically artificial, arbitrary process of naming," and he cites as an illustration the Sinbad the Sailor passage from *Ulysses*:

> Sinbad the Sailor and Tinbad the Tailor and Jinbad the Jailer and Whinbad the Whaler and Ninbad the Nailer and Finbad the Failer and Binbad the Bailer and Pinbad the Pailer and Minbad the Mailer and Hinbad the

Hailer and Rinbad the Railer and Dinbad the Kailer and Vinbad the
Quailer and Linbad the Yailer and Xinbad the Phthailer. (17.2322–2326)

Unaware that characters named Tinbad the Tailor and Whinbad the
Whaler appeared in nineteenth-century productions of *Sinbad the Sailor*
pantomimes (Herr 122), Burelbach notes simply that Joyce plays with
names alphabetically in this section, much like Charles Dickens, who,
in *Bleak House*, "rings the changes on Lord Boodle's name through
Coodle, Doodle, Foodle all the way to Noodle" ("Inquiry" 206). This
seems to be what Stephen does to Mulligan's name for the short while
that Mulligan is present in the library. At various points in the narrative
of Scylla and Charybdis, Stephen refers to Buck as *Cuck Mulligan*
(9.1025), *Puck Mulligan* (9.1125, 9.1142), and *Monk Mulligan* (9.773).
Even the self-made appellation *Ballocky Mulligan* (9.1176), which Mulligan appends to his *Honeymoon in the Hand* creation, is an onomastic
rhyme of sorts, since it is "two dactyls" like his "absurd" name that he
mocks in Telemachus (1.41). The same sort of alphabetical and comic
nameplay has its counterpart in *Finnegans Wake* in the "Some apt him
Arth, some bapt him Barth, Coll, Noll, Soll, Will, Weel, Wall" section,
for example, that precedes "The Ballad of Persse O'Reilly" (*FW* 44.12–
13). Surely as a comic device any list of names, whether it is Rabelaisian
in scope and temperament or not, successfully fragments a character
into pieces so tiny, so minute, so dependent, that the reader realizes
that the names cannot accurately reflect the character's personality.
Lists of names, particularly alphabetically generated ones such as the
reader finds in *Ulysses* and *Finnegans Wake*, are anti-erudite; they are
lists that develop ad infinitum into allusive and hyperbolic catalogues;
they are lists that, because their contents appear absurd and arbitrary,
can only be taken as anti-lists; and therein lies their humor. It is a humor of exhaustion, John Barth might say, and it is precisely this sort of
humor that prevails among the lists of names of pubs, mamafesta titles,
children's games, and so forth, that are generated in the *Wake*.

　　In addition to the alphabetical play that characterizes naming in
Scylla and Charybdis, nominal metamorphosis also distinguishes this
episode from the others in *Ulysses*. Thus, Eglinton moves from *littlejohn*
(9.367) to *littlejohn Eglinton* (9.368) to *John sturdy Eglinton* (9.660) to *Second Eglinton* (9.718) to *Besteglinton* (9.728) to *ugling Eglinton* (9.735–36) to
Steadfast John (9.737) to *Eglintonus Chronolologos* (9.811) to *eglantine*
(9.873) to *Mageeglinjohn* (9.900) to *Judge Eglinton* (9.1017) to *Eglinton Jo-*

hannes (9.1061) to *John Eclecticon* (9.1070) to *the chinless Chinaman! Chin Chon Eg Lin Ton* (9.1129). The curious Chinese rendering of Eglinton's name may owe its invention to a mid-nineteenth, twentieth-century catchphrase "John Chinaman," a derogatory phrase used to denote an ignorant Chinese. The term was well used, but short lived, and it was obsolete by the 1940s (Partridge 625). The names of Mulligan, Best, and Lyster suffer similar fates: Mulligan is named seven times in the episode—*Malachi* (9.369, 9.1056, 9.1099), *Monk Mulligan* (9.773), *Sonmulligan* (9.875), *Buckmulligan* (9.906), *Cuck Mulligan* (9.1025), *Puck Mulligan* (9.1125, 9.1143), and *Ballocky Mulligan* (9.1176)—Best is named four times—*Mr Secondbest Best* (9.714–15), *Besteglinton* (9.728), *beautifulinsadness Best* (9.735), and *Best Best*, that is, "Best of Best brothers. Good, better, best" (9.960)—and Lyster, only once—*Quakerlyster* (9.918). A prevalent theme of *Finnegans Wake*, nominal metamorphosis as it is practiced in Scylla and Charybdis is not only a means of ascribing to misbehaving characters bastardy; as an exercise of revenge, it is very much in line with the underlying theme of *Hamlet* in the episode. John Bishop points out that the centrality of *Hamlet* in *Ulysses*, comparable to the centrality of Homer, allows us to read the book not as a twentieth-century epic but as a modern revenge-play, noting that it was certainly taken that way by readers in Dublin. The coupling of naming and revenge is nothing peculiar to Scylla and Charybdis—indeed, throughout *Ulysses*, and in *Stephen Hero*, *A Portrait*, and *Finnegans Wake*, names are manipulated in Senecan fashion, and are characterized by the namer's bombast rhetoric and hyperbole.

Importantly, two of the names in Scylla and Charybdis are pseudonyms—George Russell's eonian name *AE* and Magee's pen name *Eglinton*—but they are not exempted from Stephen's onomastic dumbshow. "Mummed in names: A. E., eon: Magee, John Eglinton" (9.412), Stephen thinks. He fuses the real and assumed name of Eglinton in the portmanteau *Mageeglinjohn* (9.900), a creative composite of Eglinton's multiple identities, and a name that disregards the "sanctity" of Eglinton's pseudonym since it reveals the man behind the name, or the name behind the name. As a pseudonym, *Eglinton* is an important one because the name is void of any Celtic suggestion. John Eglinton's real name, *William Kirkpatrick Magee*, resounds with "the Celtic note," and might be a name that Little Chandler would envy. In *Dubliners*, Thomas Chandler bemoans the fact that his name is not Irish enough, and thinks that it might impede an onslaught of English critics eager to review his book of poems. He thinks, "It was a pity his name was not more Irish-looking. Perhaps it would be better to insert his mother's name before the surname: Thomas Malone Chandler, or better still: T. Malone Chandler" (D 74). Eglinton's pseudonym has an opposite effect, since it does not reinforce the Irishness of Magee's name but erases it, instead, eliminating, even purging, the name of its Celtic aurality. It is of some thematic consequence that both Eglinton and Chandler are referred to in the narratives as "little": Eglinton is twice named *littlejohn* (U 9.367, 9.368) and Thomas Chandler is "called Little Chandler because, though he was slightly under the average stature, he gave one the idea of being a little man" (D 70). The coincidence is an important one, since both men select pseudonyms that drape their nationalities, making their names appear more, or less, Irish than they are, thereby misrepresenting their racial identities.

Brook Thomas notes that when a character gives himself a pseudonym, "he affirms his basic autonomy. By becoming his own namer, he tries to become the author of his own destiny" (117). Joyce, of course, gave himself an amusing variety of pseudonyms, according to Richard Ellmann: *Aujey* (159), *James Overman* (162), *Stephen Daedalus* (164), *W. B. Yeats* (159), and *Monico Colesser* (638) number among the handful of adopted names Joyce used to sign reviews, songs, and letters, as well as the lesser-known pseudonym *Chanel*, according to Atkinson's *Dictionary of Literary Pseudonyms* (80). Brenda Maddox notes that Joyce recalled a dream in which he gave a young woman a letter pseudonymously signed *"Ulysses"* (186). He also used his friend's name, *MacGinty*, as a pseudonym (S. Joyce, *My Brother's Keeper* 105), and even referred to himself and Nora as *"Mr and Mrs Ditto MacAnaspey"* in his letters, a name echoed in Cyclops during the ordering of a round of drinks:

> —Give it a name, citizen, says Joe.
> —Wine of the country, says he.
> —What's yours? says Joe.
> —Ditto MacAnaspey, says I.
> —Three pints, Terry, says Joe.

> (U 12.143–47)

Joyce even had a name for his penis. In unpublished correspondence between him and Gogarty, Joyce sought Gogarty's advice on treatments for venereal disease, referring to the ailment and discomfort of his penis, *Ellwood* (Ferris "Untold Biography" 7).[3] Joyce's penchant for pseudonymity, albeit playful at times, is like Russell's, Magee's, and Chandler's attempts to break with the father through pseudonymity, attempts to shape for themselves a separate destiny. Similarly, Stephen's efforts to rename his library audience are attempts to author the destinies of those three who surround him.

Pseudonymity and nameplay constitute only one element of what is going on in the library on 16 June 1904. Nominal markers, in fact, lead readers to discover correlations between the characters in Stephen's audience and those characters discussed in his lecture. It is possible to work out a correlation between Stephen's audience and Shakespeare's three brothers, Edmund, Gilbert, and Richard, for example, especially since Stephen equates Best, Eglinton, and Mulligan with Shakespeare's brothers through his use of names in the episode. Best, for example, can be equated with Richard because he shares the same prenom, and since he specifically asks that his name, *Richard*, be kept "clean," calling attention himself to the coincidence of similar names:

> BEST
> That is my name, Richard, don't you know. I hope you are going to say a good word for Richard, don't you know, for my sake.
> 　　　　(*laughter*) . . .
> 　I hope Edmund is going to catch it. I don't want Richard, my name . . . . .
> 　　　　(*laughter*)
>
> 　　　　　　　　　　　　　　　　　　　　　(*U* 9.903–17)

Stephen further reinforces the association when he names Richard "*Secondbest Best*" (9.714–15), a reference that unites him with the legend of Shakespeare's "will," with his infamous "secondbest bed." Richard Shakespeare was also the youngest of William's three brothers, having been born in 1574, and Joyce aligns Richard Best with Shakespeare's third brother when he mockingly ascribes to Richard two siblings in the phrase "Best of Best brothers. Good, better, best" (9.960). John Eglinton, on the other hand, can be connected with Gilbert Shakespeare, since Gilbert was the bachelor, a fact that corresponds with one of the names given to Eglinton in the chapter: "Eglinton Johannes, of arts a bachelor" (9.1061). Indeed, Mulligan corroborates Eglinton's bachelorhood when he trolls, "*—John Eglinton, my jo, John, / Why won't you wed a wife?*" (9.1126–1127). Gilbert Shakespeare was the literate bachelor brother; he could write, and his signature survives as witness to a property lease in March 1610 (Palmers 219). Moreover, Eglinton's "elder's gall" (9.19) also aligns him with Gilbert, since after William, Gilbert was the eldest brother, born in 1566. The counterpart of Shakespeare's third brother, Edmund, is more carefully hidden in Joyce's chapter, though he corresponds to the noisiest and most animated character in the novel—Buck Mulligan. Edmund Shakespeare, born 1580, was an actor like his oldest brother, a "mummer," as Mulligan refers to the tradesmen. A character in *King Lear*, Edmund is the Machiavellian bastard son, and whenever Stephen alludes to *Lear* in his thoughts, he does so to counterblast one of Mulligan's incipient jests (9.461, 9.911–12, 9.1026, 9.1162) or to respond to Mulligan in some other way, as when Stephen thinks of Cordelia's hanging (orchestrated by Edmund) when he learns that Mulligan and Haines have been invited to George Moore's party without him (9.314). Stephen argues in Scylla and Charybdis that Shakespeare's nominal revenge takes a variety of forms: he hides his own fair name in the sonnets, he uses real names from the chronicles, and he makes his brothers villains and nasty uncles. During his lecture, however, Stephen proves to be just as wily as the Bard himself, making his audience part of the insidious literary history he discusses, and "Mak[ing] them accomplices" (9.158) at the same time. If Joyce wanted to get the better of Shakespeare, as Nora's remark to Budgen suggests, then he succeeds here, since by reconstructing Shakespeare's brothers, he calls "them into life across the waters of Lethe" (14.1113–1114); and as the poor ghosts troop to his call, he triumphantly supplants Shakespeare as brother, father, son, ghost, and creator.

Flann O'Brien claims that Joyce made a career out of revenge and retribution, noting that Joyce gets even not by replicating in ceaseless fashion the enemies in his life, creating, for example, countless Gogartys, Byrnes, or Westons; rather, O'Brien explains, Joyce punishes his enemies by duplicating himself over and over again: "Joyce spent a lifetime establishing himself as a character in fiction" (326), O'Brien notes, and he reconstructs that character anew in each new work. But Joyce's self-replication is tied not merely to narcissism or only to revenge but to his theories of paternity and creation. And what O'Brien sees as Joyce's egocentric "twinning" allows him to recreate life out of life, a vocation he espoused in *A Portrait* (*P* 172), and one he attributes admiringly to Shakespeare when he says that Shakespeare "drew Shylock out of his own long pocket" (*U* 9.741–42). In fact, O'Brien, too, is guilty of establishing Joyce as a character in fiction, since the unnamed, unclean, unshaven writer-protagonist of his 1939 *At Swim-Two-Birds* is suggestive of Stephen Dedalus. In his essay "A Bash in the Tunnel," O'Brien writes:

> Joyce created, in narcissus fashion, the ageless Stephen. Beginning with importing real characters into his books, he achieves the magnificent inversion of making them legendary and fictional. It is quite preposterous. Thousands of people believe that there once lived a man named Sherlock Holmes. (326)

O'Brien credits Joyce with doing exactly what Stephen credits Shakespeare with doing: both men take real people and transform them into literary magnificoes, while their fictional characters take on a magnitude larger than life. It is the ultimate revenge, in that it condemns a real person to caricatured fabrication.

Gogarty was one of Joyce's "characters" who was infuriated by Joyce's use of him, as well as his irreverent "Ballad of Joking Jesus." Gogarty's revenge against Joyce, as might be expected, follows Shakespeare's, in that he makes Joyce a character in his fiction, veiling his name in his writings, punning on Joyce's surname, and condemning Joyce to infamy because "he was not a gentlemen, his education was second-rate and he had a diseased mind," according to Richard Wall, who details Gogarty's systematic revenge against Joyce in his fiction. But for all of Gogarty's hostility, he may have appreciated late in life that as Joyce's Buck Mulligan he "had already achieved a measure of immortality, even if the form of that immortality was not exactly to his liking" (Wall 93). Stephen's nominal revenge has the same end result. As linguistic deformation, as rhetorical revenge, as manipulative onomastics, Stephen's semantic maneuverings succeed in ascribing to his library audience an imperishable fame. Shakespeare, of course, resorted to a similar strategy, citing as the creative force behind many of the sonnets his desire to bestow immortality on his lover, as the final couplet of "Shall I compare thee to a summer's day" suggests: "So long as men can breathe or eyes can see, / So long lives this, and this gives life to thee." As a means of retributive immortality, Stephen uses naming and nameplay to render his friends, his enemies, and his rivals immortal—not only so that they might live forever in infamy, but so that he may reuse them, refashion them and regurgitate them at will in his fiction, endlessly generating them at his own discretion and for his own bizarre pleasure in an act of never-ending literary paternity. Using names to bastardize and emasculate his audience, and to point to similarities between cultural and historical figures, Stephen's treatment of onomastics in the Scylla and Charybdis episode is an intellectual exercise that involves linguistic, political, and academic razzle-dazzle, a magnificence silently aimed at an unsuspecting literate and cerebral audience.

CHAPTER FIVE

Naming and Identity

One-third of the way through F. Scott Fitzgerald's *The Great Gatsby*, Nick Carraway supplies the reader with the names of some of Gatsby's regular guests, saying,

> Once I wrote down on the empty space of a time-table the names of those who came to Gatsby's house that summer. It is an old time-table now, disintegrating at its folds, and headed, "This schedule in effect July 5th, 1922." But I can still read the gray names, and they will give you a better impression than my generalities of those who accepted Gatsby's hospitality and paid him the subtle tribute of knowing nothing whatever about him. (61)

The list continues for six paragraphs, spanning three pages of text, and enumerating seventy-six names. An objective listing so far as Carraway is concerned, one that arranges the names cartographically, dividing them into East Egg and West Egg contingents, the catalogue of names offers a clear impression of the nature of the guests. Yet Fitzgerald's list is also a comical one, and like so many of Joyce's, it gets its comedy from nominal juxtaposition.

One paragraph, for example, contains a handful of thalassic, nautical names sandwiched in between the names of less piscatological guests. The *Fishguards*, the *Hammerheads*, the *Ripley Snells*, the *Whitebaits*, and the *Belugas*, for example, are buried in a paragraph that contains eight other names, names that are comical of their own accord—the *Stonewall Jackson Abrams*, or the *Dancies*, the *Endives*, or the *Ulysses Swetts* (62). Fitzgerald's nominal thematics are as important as Joyce's, and his use of onomastics—indeed, his assurance that names could paint a better portrait than he—is important to our understanding of naming and identity, since the very names of the guests seem to justify,

109

if not demand, their continued attendance at Gatsby's fashionable parties. The *Chester Beckers*, the *Willie Voltaires*, the *Dennickers*, the *O. R. P. Schraeders, Cecil Roebuck, Cecil Shoen, Doctor Webster Civet,* and *Newton Orchid* (a name reminiscent of Newton's fruitful discovery in the orchard)—these are some of the names of the partygoers, and although none is described in physical terms, and none in psychological terms, the reader can sense these things from the names alone, since names often contain a wealth of telescoped information about a person's ancestry, religion, social class, physical appearance, and ethnic tradition.

We are often guided unconsciously in our readings of names, what we glean from names, and how we negotiate between name and character. Mary Seeman discusses a recent advertising campaign that utilized onomastic research, hoping to capitalize on a public awareness of naming traditions. The technique attempted to appeal to a wide audience through the use of a variety of names but the effort backfired unwittingly. Seeman explains:

> In the summer of 1977, the Ontario Human Rights' Commission displayed an advertisement in the province's public transit vehicles. It read:
>> For Pete's sake, for Juanita's sake,
>> For Horst's sake, for Liv's sake,
>> For Dmitri's sake, for Maria's sake,
>> For Nadia's sake, for Chi Ming's sake,
>> For Aziz's sake, for Sol's sake,
>> For everybody's sake, let's work together.
>
> The ethnic diversity of the names made the message comprehensible. So comprehensible was it, in fact, that the French-speaking population of Ontario immediately protested at not being represented. It was evident that none of the names was French. How was it that a short word, often of one syllable only, is able to encode enough information to "stand for" a whole ethnic tradition? ("Name and Identity" 129)

Seeman's point is well taken, and one that would not be lost on writers like Fitzgerald whose onomastic play reveals his interest in naming and identity. Joyce, too, reveals such an interest in naming and identity, an interest he most notably exhibits in the name of his artist-figure, *Dedalus*. To be sure, dozens of characters whose names typify their sensibilities walk through Joyce's fiction, but Dedalus is probably the most obvious example of an "encoded" name. Most Joyceans know that in

the Greek, *Daedalus* means "cunningly wrought." Like Stephen himself, then, Stephen Dedalus's nominal precursor was driven by a name
that defined him: the Daedalus name was as much an aptonym for the
labyrinth maker as it is for Stephen the artist, whose "silence, exile and
cunning" will stand him in good stead. For both men, it is a name that
reeks of nominal determinism. Of course, the name *Daedalus* may have
been appended to the Greek artisan *because* of his skills; that is, the
name may have been bestowed on him retroactively, ex post facto, as it
were—and this is an important problem, since, when it comes to
names and naming, we frequently find ourselves pondering a sort of
"what came first, the chicken or the egg?" question, and often, we cannot tell.

    In literature, as in life, a person or character is often given a name
that, upon examination, may seem to have a telling or amusing relationship to his or her personality, appearance, or job. In Scylla and
Charybdis, for example, Eglinton assumes that it is Stephen's name
that influences his ready wit and methodical temperament, saying,
"Your own name is strange enough. I suppose it explains your fantastical humour" (9.949–50). Had John Eglinton been an onomastician, he
might have noted that Stephen's surname was an aptonym. Emery
Walker has recently published a list of aptonyms in the *American Name
Society Bulletin* (7), and although Walker's collection numbers in the
hundreds, he lists only a few dozen. The following is a brief selection:
John Law, a policeman; *Jay Lipps*, a trumpet player; *Julie Yellin*, a
cheerleader; *Stanford Schwimer*, a member of the swim team at Stanford;
and *Juan Trippe*, ex-president of Pan Am Airlines. Some onomasticians
argue that every name is an aptonym, and that "for every Name there is
A Story" (Cornog and Perper 379). In many ways, I think, Joyce
thought the same thing, especially since much of his nameplay targets
and victimizes the names of contemporary or historical persons or
wields a pointed lancet at the names of his fictional characters.

    "You will say those names were already in the chronicles from which
he took the stuff of his plays," Stephen says in Scylla and Charybdis,
anticipating his audience's objection to his theory of Shakespeare's
onomastic revenge. Stephen's rhetorical reply is as appropriate to an
examination of Joyce's nameplay as it is to Shakespeare's, since with
Stephen, we wonder, "Why did he take them rather than others?"
(9.983–84). Joyce's use of "appropriate" names is what is of interest in
this chapter, not so much his use of real or fabricated names. Propriety,

in other words, not plausibility. Richard Ellmann notes that Dubliners walked around in trepidation after the publication of *Ulysses* asking each other "Are you in it?" or "Am I in it?" (364), seeking traces of themselves and one another in Joyce's characters. That Joyce used real names of real people is of little concern to this chapter; rather, it is the motivating force behind his onomastic selection that is important to our understanding of Joyce's philosophy of naming, particularly as it applies to concepts of naming and identity.

Joyce writes in *Finnegans Wake* that "when a part so ptee does duty for the holos we soon grow to use of an allforabit" (18.36–19.02). I suggest that a name is a small, petit (ptee) part for the whole, an "all" for a "bit," and that Joyce uses names as a form of shorthand, turning a name, an onomastic morpheme, into the ultimate metaphor of character. What I would like to discuss in this chapter are the ways that naming not only influences one's social position, one's economic status, one's occupation, and one's character evaluation, but how naming affects livelihood, temperament, physiognomy, and characterization.

Tom Stoppard refers to this onomastic phenomenon as the Cognomen Syndrome in his 1972 play *Jumpers,* and describes it as a general sense of direction brought about by a person's surname:

> BONES: [*Introducing himself*] Inspector Bones, C. I. D.
>
> ARCHIE: Bones . . . ? I had a patient named Bones. I wonder if he was any relation?—an osteopath.
>
> BONES: My brother!
>
> ARCHIE: Remember the case well. Cognomen Syndrome. My advice to him was to take his wife's maiden name of Foot and carry on from there.
>
> BONES: He took your advice but unfortunately he got interested in chiropody. He is now in an asylum near Uxbridge.
>
> ARCHIE: Isn't that interesting? I must write him up. The Cognomen Syndrome is my baby, you know.
>
> BONES: You discovered it?
>
> ARCHIE: I've got it. Jumper's the name—my card. . . .
>   I can still jump over seven feet. . . . Long jump. My main interest, however, is the trampoline.
>
>   (61)

As Stoppard's characters suggest, naming very often influences identity—and not always for absurd or comedic purposes, either.

Jumpers is a murder mystery, for example. Since so many of Joyce's characters suffer from what Stoppard identifies as the Cognomen Syndrome—characters such as *Stephen* and *Simon Dedalus, Rody Kickham, Cecil Thunder, Nasty Roche, Heron, Milly Bloom, Andrew Horne, Earwicker / Porter, Shem, Shaun, Issy,* the *Doyle* jurors, and a host of characters in *Dubliners*—a categoric examination of the names and identities of a number of characters can inform a variety of critical approaches to Joyce's onomastics.

One might begin at the beginning, by examining the title of Joyce's first novel, *Stephen Hero*. Stanislaus claims in his diary entry for 2 February 1904, that he suggested the title to Joyce. The entry also reveals that he and his brother made fun of the names of some of Joyce's characters, changing them and "rechristening" them to reap comic consequence:

> He [Jim] has not decided on a title, and again I made most of the suggestions. Finally a title of mine was accepted: "Stephen Hero," from Jim's own name in the book "Stephen Dedalus." The title, like the book, is satirical. Between us we rechristened the characters, calling them by names which seemed to suit their tempers or which suggested the part of the country from which they had come.

From Joyce's earliest literary attempts, then, his use of onomastics borders on the opportunistic, using names to indicate personality, social class, and locality of birth, christening his characters with names that "suit their tempers." As Stanislaus notes, the title *Stephen Hero* mocks the name and self-adopted vocation of the protagonist Stephen Daedalus. *Hero*, then, does not necessarily function as a surname in the title of the novel, although many readers might appropriately assume that it does. What Joyce does to the Daedalus name in the title is similar to what Jacques Derrida notes of Jean Genet in *Glas;* that is, he turns the proper name into a common noun so that he might pun on it and extract further meaning from its manipulated forms (11). The name gets fractured and refractured throughout the work. Since *Daedalus* cannot be converted into a common noun, Joyce replaces the surname with a noun that Stephen would approve of—*hero;* thus, the title remains self-reflexive while at the same time it introduces a disguised onomastic pun from the point of view of the "hero" himself.

Jonathan Culler, discussing names and puns, recounts the literary history that Stephen notes in Scylla and Charybdis when he asserts that Shakespeare "has hidden his own name, a fair name, William, in the plays, a super here, a clown there" (9.921–22). Culler writes,

> Shakespeare, whose sonnets ring the changes on *Will,* Francis Ponge, whose sponges Jacques Derrida has brought to the surface, or John Donne, whose name was always poised to become a participle, all illustrate what Derrida . . . has called "the patient, stealthy, quasi-animal or vegetable, tireless, monumental, derisory transformation of one's name, a rebus, into a thing or name of a thing." From this vantage, literature can be seen not as an author's appropriation of the world but as a dissemination or dispersal of the proper name, the transformation of it into the elements of a world—in short, a foundation of letters. (10)

Culler argues that the literary act is an act of nominal immortality, and, as Stephen argues in Scylla and Charybdis, it is an act of self-replication, an act in which the author always meets himself. Unlike the artist's offspring, over whom he has little, if any, control, whom "he will see . . . [as] grotesque attempts of nature to foretell or to repeat himself" (9.434–35), the artist is able to control the reproduction of his image in literature (though not the unpredictable, interpretive whims of his readers), even though he cannot do so in nature. "So does the artist weave and unweave his image," Stephen explains in the National Library (9.377–78). Stephen "hero," then, is one such replication of the artist.

Many of the modernists were successful in their attempt to redefine the concept of hero by casting themselves or their contemporaries in the heroic role. Yeats's poems on Parnell, his "Easter 1916," and his poems on Lady Gregory and her son Major Robert Gregory; Pound's self-drawn Mauberly figure; Eliot's pensive speaker in *Four Quartets;* H. D.'s *Hermione,* her Helen; Sitwell's privatized World War I poetry; Woolf's polyphonous narrative voices; Hemingway's Nick Adams; Wolfe's Eugene Gant; and Stein's biographical and autobiographical works, for example—all these are attempts at redefining the concept of "hero" and redesigning twentieth-century assumptions about what constitutes heroism. Joyce's Dedalus is much the same, though like H. D.'s. Helen, he is drawn from legend. Stephen's namesake Daedalus invented the plumb-line, the axe, and the saw; he discovered glue; he was the first to understand the importance of masts and sails. The epitome of a great craftsman, there was no challenge Daedalus could not meet. Surely, he was a hero to Queen Pasiphae, since he constructed for her the false cow; but what sort of construction is Stephen capable of? And how heroic is this modern namesake of Daedalus?

The incongruity of Stephen's Daedalean name is heightened when set against the backdrop of Dublin, and becomes a recurring subject of conjecture for characters in Joyce's work. Early in *A Portrait*, for example, the name is questioned:

> —What is your name?
> Stephen had answered:
> —Stephen Dedalus.
> Then Nasty Roche had said:
> —What kind of a name is that?
> And when Stephen had not been able to answer Nasty Roche had asked:
> —What is your father?
> Stephen had answered:
> —A gentleman.
>
> (9)

Part of the humor of this passage comes from its irony: "What kind of a name is that?" is no sort of question for someone named Nasty Roche to be asking. Of course, it is important that Stephen is "not able to answer" Roche's inquiry; nor does he properly respond to his next question. Stephen's misunderstanding of Roche's second question is also amusing, since Stephen does not realize that Roche is questioning his father's nationality. "What is your father?" is an appropriate question to ask a namesake of Daedalus, and Stephen's reply—"a gentleman"—indicates not only his innocence of youth but his ignorance of language, as well.

Like the mythical Daedalus, Stephen's father constructs for him a false cow; he creates out of language a moocow for baby tuckoo (*P* 7), a story John Joyce often repeated to his son James, as we learn in Joyce's birthday letter from his father dated 31 January 1931:

> I wonder do you recollect the old days in Brighton Square, when you were Babie Tuckoo, and I used to take you out in the Square and tell you all about the moo-cow that used to come down from the mountain and take little boys across? (*Letters* 3.212)

According to Gifford, the moocow story still survives in the West of Ireland:

the supernatural (white) cow takes children across to an island realm
where they are relieved of the petty restraints and dependencies of childhood and magically schooled as heroes before they are returned to their
astonished parents and community. (*Joyce Annotated* 133)

Baby Tuckoo's return as hero may be reflected in the title *Stephen Hero*,
but more important is the transformation that occurs away from home,
in exile, as it were.

In the playground scene of *A Portrait* where Nasty Roche interro-
gates Stephen, Stephen is onomastically surrounded by aptonyms.
First, there is *Rody Kickham*, a decent fellow who plays a fine game of
football, a game where advancing the ball is done by "kicking it or
striking it with the hand" (Gifford *Joyce Annotated* 135). Kickham plays
well: "he would be captain of the third line all the fellows said" (*P* 8).
True to his surname, then, Rody Kickham is a good kicker: his name is
an aptonym. The name *Cecil Thunder* is an aptonym, as well. Thunder is
the sort of boy who would "give you a toe in the rump" (also a kicker),
according to *Cantwell*, a boy who, himself, "can't" fight, but one who
advertises his friend Cecil's thunderous temper (*P* 9). In Stephen's little
playground, the earliest away-from-home microcosm in *A Portrait*, all
of the boys' names define them. Kickham kicks; Nasty is nasty; Thunder thunders; and Cantwell can't.[1] The name of Stephen's infirm friend
Athy is important, too, since the boy's name is presented to Stephen as
an answer to a riddle, as if the name were a mystery, bearing some sort
of secret knowledge—indeed, he doesn't even identify the riddle as a
name riddle, but says it is an "old" riddle (*P* 25), as it is, since his variety
of riddle, the traditional conundrum, is closely related to the formulaic
"true riddle," as Patrick McCarthy explains in *The Riddles of "Finnegans
Wake"* (18). Importantly, Athy is comfortable enough with his name to
pun on it, but in contrast, Stephen knows no such nominal comfort. As
son of Dedalus, Stephen even incurs an implied name, too, that of
Icarus, and his associations with Icarian flight and fall become the subject of nominal inquiry and musing throughout Joyce's canon. While
Stephen's schoolmates in *A Portrait* have "grown into" their names,
Stephen, as yet, has not. He spends all of *A Portrait* and most of *Ulysses*
trying to negotiate the legacy of his name, and trying to account for the
fact that in twentieth-century Ireland, "artist" is no longer a synonym
for "hero."

Joyce believed there was a magical relationship between names and identity. In a letter to Stanislaus two months after his son was born, Joyce wrote that Giorgio, referred to as "the child" by Joyce and "little—what's his name" by Stani (*Letters* 2:100, 104), had been given no name yet, and that such a decision was a difficult one:

> The child has got no name yet, though he will be two months old on Thursday next. He is very fat and very quiet. I don't know who he's like. . . . He seems to be very healthy in spite of his paternal inheritance. I think a child should be allowed to take his father's or mother's name at will on coming of age. (*Letters* 2:107–8)

A serious believer in the appropriateness of names, Joyce chose names as carefully for his characters as he did for his children, often questioning, in fact, the relevance of his choices: he wrote to Stanislaus in July 1905 to complain about Nora's depression, afraid that it would affect the humor of his soon-to-be-born child, saying, "I do not know what strange morose creature she will bring forth after all her tears and I am even beginning to reconsider the appositeness of the names I had chosen ('George' and 'Lucy')" (*Letters* 2:95).

With his musings about the appropriateness of names, Joyce would no doubt appreciate a recent installment of the popular "Wizard of Id" cartoon, since it hints at issues directly related to his philosophy of naming. A sign hanging outside a stable reads, "Stable boy wanted." A young boy approaches to apply for the job and when the foreman asks his name he answers, "Scoop." "You're hired," says the foreman, smiling. Parker's cartoon is a humorous illustration of the subjects of this chapter, naming and identity, since the comic strip seems to question whether names are "conventional" or "natural." Many of the names of Joyce's characters are conventional, since Joyce was so often driven by his poetics of verisimilitude; but a large enough percentage have "natural" names, names that bear a direct correlation to the character's role in the plot. When John Joyce learned of Nora Barnacle's surname, for example, he remarked with amusement that she'd never leave Joyce. Often the correlation between names in fiction is amusing, too, as in the name of *Andrew Horne,* whose surname makes him a natural for Joyce's fertility chapter where "Horne's Hall" becomes an eponym for the Lying-in Hospital. The actual doctor in charge of the National Maternity Hospital, Andrew Horne had his name boldly emblazoned across the entry to the hospital. None could miss the name, and few could overlook its suggestiveness, least of all Joyce. Aside from the phallic undertones of the name *Horne*, like those suggested by Stephen's schoolmates who name *Tusker Boyle* "Tusker," Joyce also may have found the name irresistibly appropriate for his "Oxen" chapter since it carries a serendipitous bovine pun.

Like the name *Horne*, names are suggestive—yet even nameless characters in Joyce are able to suggest connections and correspondences. Admittedly, it is ironic that a character without a name can maintain an allusiveness, but this is precisely the case in the name of Mangan's sister, the object of desire in "Araby." Though nameless, Mangan's sister suggests the romantic and nationalist poet James Clarence Mangan (1803–1849), author of the popular "Dark Rosaleen." Like the subject of Mangan's poem, Ireland herself, the girl in "Araby" is iconized; she is idolized, made out to be larger than life, and the boy is consumed by his adoration of her, much like the speaker in Mangan's poem:

> I could scale the blue air,
> I could plough the high hills,
> Oh, I could kneel all night in prayer . . .
> And one beamy smile from you
> Would float like light between
> My toils and me, my own, my true,
> My Dark Rosaleen.
>
> (Gifford *Joyce Annotated* 44)

As a name, "Mangan's sister" tells the reader a lot without telling her or him anything. It is one of Joyce's shorthand names, an encoded name, a name that "stands for" an unarticulated something. Paradoxically, the missing name is "readable."

Mangan's sister is nameless, like the "Nameless One" of *Ulysses;* but their namelessness condemns neither to indeterminacy. Rather, as Daniel Ferrer says of the name of the Nameless One in "Characters in *Ulysses,*" "the absence of a name tends to become a name; the absence of features, a characteristic feature" (150), as in Beckett's *The Unnamable,* where the lack of a name becomes a special kind of name, or in Jean Rhys's *Good Morning, Midnight,* where the truculent boss is named *Mr. Blank,* hardly a name at all. Ferrer calls such practice a "radical undermining" of nominalization, but it is an onomastic coup on Joyce's part.

If, as Bloom thinks in Aeolus, "everything speaks in its own way" (*U* 7.177), then names, too, can be vocal—even in their absence.

While namelessness is a common fate for Joyce's characters, similarities between names is another cause for inspection, as in the case of *Milly*, a name that Bloom notes is the same as *Molly* "watered down" (*U* 6.87). As Michael Ragussis explains in *Acts of Naming*, a child's name indicates the parents' desires; and the fact that the daughter is named like the mother is quite a significant onomastic indicator:

> The child enters the naming system as unpredictable, unfixable, the power that threatens to resist our will or wish. The child is always potentially the deviant, the break in the chain, the hole in history, for the . . . family. For this reason, the family name functions to classify—and thereby nullify—the individual, while the proper name exerts the power of a magical wish which expresses the will of the family. No names better illustrate this latter point than those which Puritan parents commonly gave: Experience, Waitstill, Preserved, Hopestill, Wait, Thanks, Desire, Unite and Supply. Other appellations included Rich Grace, More Mercy, Relieve, Believe, Reform, Deliverance and Strange. Both the family name and the proper name form part of a system whose function is to determine and fix the child's identity, to make the child serve the will of the family. (7)

Surely this seems the motivating force behind the Blooms' choice of name for Milly. Bloom and Molly apparently want another version of Molly, and their naming attests to that, Bloom perhaps out of incest, and Molly perhaps out of vanity.

Milly, in fact, has grown to be just like Molly. Molly notes in Penelope, "I was just like that myself" (*U* 18.1077–1078) when she recalls Milly's displays of impudence; and she notes that Milly's habit of cocking her legs up "on the windowsill before all the people passing they all look at her" reminds her of herself: "like me when I was her age" (18.1035–1036), she thinks. In addition, Milly even aspires to look like her mother, and Molly notes that "shes always making love to my things too the few old rags I have wanting to put her hair up at 15 my powder too" (18.1063–1064). Further, Milly imitates her mother's singing by whistling her arias while flirting with the Devans boys (18.1024). Milly is a younger version of Molly—someone who acts, behaves, dresses, and looks like Molly because her name wills it. Again, if we recall Bloom's revelation in Circe that Milly was called *Marionette* (15.540), we can see how through naming, Milly is considered not only a smaller version of Molly (Marion) but an impressionable and maneuverable "puppet"—a "marionette"—as well.

The similarities between mother and daughter are not lost on Bloom, either, who Molly notes talks more to the daughter than he talks to her, even helping her on with her coat, as if Molly were "finished out and laid on the shelf" (18.1022). Molly argues that Milly seems to flirt with Bloom, since she pretends to a fascination when her father explains things to her from out of the paper, "pretending to understand," Molly notes, adding, "sly of course" (18.1018–1019). The choice of name for the daughter, then, because of its orthographical similarity to the name Molly, reveals the Blooms' desire to predict through naming the unpredictable, to fix through naming the unfixable—they want to control the daughter, to "nullify" her, as Ragussis argues, and they arrive at this control through onomastic fixity.

Similar to the Cognomen Syndrome, Milly's sense of direction comes from her given name, one deliberately chosen to ensure the continued youth of the mother who sees her young self in the daughter, and the ceaseless virility of the father who sees in the daughter the prospect of renewed sexual vigor. In addition, Milly's near-error, the fact that she was "on the pop of writing Blazes Boylan's" (4.408) in her letter to Bloom, aligns her through accidental circumstance with her mother's lover, and further suggests the displacement of the mother by the daughter.

Importantly, Joyce's use of "natural" names does not reduce his characters to types, making someone nothing more than a product of her or his name, even though the concept of "natural" names is one that our imaginations, and Joyce's, might find irresistible. Invariably, important characters in fiction are given a host of names, a series of names that function as a composite of the "true" name. The point is not so much to show how characters in a fiction are unwittingly steered by their names, but to argue that names are so essential to evaluation that outcomes are often determined on account of them. Ragussis explains:

> While fiction recharges with power the names of people, it does so most profoundly by claiming not that names are natural or that destinies are shaped by a powerful name, but that people shape destinies—others' and their own—by the immense power they accord to names. Fiction

shows us that we so value names that they become the center of both symbolic and literal acts of recognition, abandonment, rape, suicide, and murder. . . . In this light, the name functions most profoundly in fiction not as a static standard-bearer that reveals character from the beginning, but as the center of a matrix of action. (11)

Joyce subscribes to theories of naming similar to the one explained by Ragussis; but he also characteristically mocks that theory and theories like it throughout his canon, typically vacillating in his support of one theory or another. A comic example occurs in the name *miss Dubedat*, a name Bloom conjures with in Lestrygonians when he muses, "Wouldn't mind being a waiter in a swell hotel. Tips, evening dress, halfnaked ladies. May I tempt you to a little more filleted lemon sole, miss Dubedat? Yes, do bedad. And she did bedad. Huguenot name I expect that" (8.887–90). Not surprisingly, Miss Dubedat is later rendered in the text as *Miss Dubedatandshedidbedad*, as if her name controlled her behavior, as if her name willed her to be "dat."

Another place where Joyce pokes fun at his own constructs of "natural" naming is in the mock parliamentary debate in Cyclops where councilmen named *Cowe* [cow] *Conacre* and *Allfours* debate the slaughter of animals (12.860–79). Appropriately, their opponent in the debate is named *Staylewit*, an aptonym for a parliamentarian. In Cyclops, the naming reveals the characteristics of the personalities just as it predicts and informs their actions. The dog *Garryowen*, for example, most likely named after the drinking song, is subsequently referred to as *Garry*, a person's name, when the Citizen asks, "—What's on you, Garry?" (12.704) or declares, "—After him, Garry! After him, boy!" (12.1905). His name also changes to *Owen Garry* later in the chapter, suggesting his alignment with the third-century contemporary of Finn MacCool, Owen Garry (12.717). The mastiff's "human" names serve to bring about his metamorphosis in the chapter, and help to fuel the theme of cynanthropy that underlies the episode where animals are humanistic and humans are animalistic.

Joyce often pokes fun at the idea of "natural naming," and examples abound in *Ulysses* and *Finnegans Wake*. For example, HCE is named Here Comes Everybody because he "always indeed looked" like an "imposing everybody" (*FW* 32.19), we are told. Similarly, the names of those at the forest wedding in Cyclops (*U* 12.1266–1298) make their presence seem natural, if not predictable. Surely the catalogue of women's names is meant to be a comical one as Robert Scholes, Noel Riley Fitch, and the Benstocks have shown (Scholes 169–70; Fitch 353–54; Benstocks *Who's He* 218); but Andreas Palme and Fritz Senn identify important elements and puns in the catalogue of participants and guests, and note that while many of the women's names are humorous, the catalogue resounds with political allusion and with literary and historical reference (Palme 150–56; Senn "Trivia Ulysseana IV" 167). A fine example occurs in the name *Mrs. Kitty Dewey-Mosse* (*U* 12.1276). Palme dismantles the name using information gleaned from Franklyn's *Dictionary of Nicknames* (54), and places the name alongside *Ikey Mo* and *Ikey Moses*, identifying the name of *Mrs. Kitty Dewey-Mosse* in an anti-Semitic context (152): "Jewy is the inseparable nickname of any man named Moss: from the fact that many Jews, originally surnamed Moses, have become 'moss' either by deliberate change of name, or through the process of sloven pronunciation." The historical transformation from *Moses* to *Moss* makes the name a "natural" inclusion at the forest wedding; but as with other names Palme takes apart in his discussion of the chapter, Palme sees the name as having multiple meanings, and Dewey-Mosse's presence at the wedding becomes curious and covert on account of it.

Given Joyce's attitudes about the appropriateness of names, as well as his ideas about "natural" naming, the women at the forest wedding may be present because their names will or determine it. Where else would Mrs. Daphne Bays or Mrs. Clyde Twelvetrees or Lady Sylvester Elmshade be on a June afternoon? Joyce's list of women's names (as well as his use of names like "Allfours" and "Staylewit," for example) has been seen as an exhaustive catalogue of puns; instead, it might be interesting to regard the list as a commentary on onomastic theory, on "natural" naming, especially since so many readers have identified what Peter Costello says are "real enough" names within the catalogue (85).

Carl Jung, who has argued both for and against the deterministic power of names—just as he has argued both for and against *Ulysses*—concedes that there is a certain power in naming and, as a result of his observations, questions whether correlations between a person and his or her name are "whimsicalities of chance, suggestive effects of the name," or "meaningful coincidences" (427). Jung lists a handful of examples of people whose names and personalities are uncannily related, citing, as might be expected, the popular Freud/joy connection

(427), a connection Joyce exploited, since he often mused upon the meaning of the name *Freud*, boasting to friends that the name *Joyce* meant the same as Freud's. In *Finnegans Wake*, however, Joyce alters the meaning of the name *Freud* when he writes of being "yung and easily freudened" (115.22–23), thereby changing "joy" to "fear" (or fright) in a gesture of onomastic verve. Jung's queries about coincidence, whimsy, and suggestion, while important to an understanding of naming and identity, are important to an understanding of what lies at the basis of literary onomastics in particular, since authors of a text have the power to *create* for the character a correlation between him and his name, her and her name. It is an artificial process, then, this link between naming and identity when it is inscribed in literature. Names in literature tend to mirror and magnify the real-life anomalies that Jung notes in his brief discussion of names and identity; but it is interesting to see how Joyce inscribes what Jung calls "meaningful coincidences," and how Joyce mocks those same "whimsicalities of chance," often parading a system of naming he establishes in his fiction.

During Stephen's library lecture, Eglinton compliments Stephen by saying that he "makes good use of the name" (*U* 9.949). Joyce, too, makes good use of names, often incorporating into his fiction Tom Stoppard's Cognomen Syndrome, and ascribing to his characters a sense of direction based on onomastic play. In Joyce's fiction, surnames offer to their bearers a certain role which they may or may not be able or willing to fulfill. Although nominal determinism in Joyce often works, the coincidences of name and identity are often negotiable, and the tensions that result from a character's denial of a name become part of the story itself.

For example, both Bloom and Stephen, David Seed argues, are incapable of living up to their surnames: Stephen is no fabulous artisan, and Bloom, whose name has been changed in an effort to "cast off Jewish origins" (48), disguises himself under pseudonyms that etymologically and orthographically drape his racial identity. Seed concludes that both Stephen and Bloom are impostors since they do not fulfill the roles their names assign them. But Stephen warns both Bloom and the reader that names are impostors, that names often deceive, that they trigger unreliable associations.

In Joyce's canon, the reader finds a number of examples where names are not to be trusted. Names are often misspoken, misremembered or misspelled, as in *Figatner, Pendennis, L. Boom, Joe Jack Harry*

Mulvey, Bollopedoom or *Old Ollebo, M. P;* self-adopted, as in *Karoly,
Virag, Bloom, T. Malone Chandler,* or *Flower;* exclaimed expletively, as
in *Hairy Iopas!* and *Christicle!;* appended in revenge, as in *littlejohn
Eglinton;* doled out by the patriarchy, as in *Our Lady of the Cherries;* or
appended to undeserving namelings, as in the "curious coincidence"
of *Simon Dedalus,* an alleged performer in Hengler's Circus; in addition,
names often reflect an occasion of misbehavior, as in the name *uncle
Peter;* or they may reflect a momentary consanguinity. Often one name
seems to be a permutation of another, as in the names *Rudy* and *Ruby,
Purefoy* and *Beaufoy, Crofter* and *Crofton,* and *Bergan* and *Bergin,* or con-
fused, as in *Kendal Bushe* and *Seymour Bushe;* and names are often falsely
ornamented as in *Kranliberg,* an imposture that Cranly would display
outside of his pork butcher shop. Names are also allusively misleading,
as in the names *Beatrice Justice, Father Flynn,* and *Garryowen;* and they
can be amusingly rendered in a portmanteau—dozens of these exist in
Joyce. Nominal errors are often perpetuated, as well, and constitute yet
another reason why names are impostors, as in *Goulding, Collis and
Ward,* the signifier that Richie Goulding aggrandizes to make himself
seem a partner in the Collis and Ward firm, or in the repeated references to *Corless*'s restaurant even though the name of the restaurant
had been changed late in the nineteenth century. Stephen's name, of
course, is no exception, either, and may prove to be an impostor, as
well, since Stephen's literary production only amounts to "a capful of
light odes" (*U* 14.1119), according to Lynch, whose chiding painfully
reminds Stephen of his artistic potential: "The young man's face grew
dark. All could see how hard it was for him to be reminded of his promise" (14.1123–1124). Charged to "make good use of the name" (9.949),
Stephen knows he must sooner or later fulfill Mulligan's glib predic-
tion: "—Ten years, he said, chewing and laughing. He is going to write
something in ten years" (10.1089–1090). Through dramatic irony, readers know that Stephen began writing *Dubliners* that afternoon, since
the DEAR DIRTY DUBLIN section which opens his "Parable of the
Plums" not only begins with the word *Dubliners* set on a separate line
like a title but contains echoes of the opening story in Joyce's collection,
"The Sisters," a story of "Two Dublin vestals . . . elderly and pious"
(7.923).[2] The Dublin literati remain skeptical, however, and impatiently
await tangible proof of Stephen's creative faculties.

    Names are not always doled out diplomatically in literature, as
names are often ironic, cacophonic, or maleficent. Often characters

rebel against their names, a tendency that Shakespeare notes and even
encourages in *2 Henry VI*. Peter, an armorer's apprentice, is about to
fight his master when the Earl of Salisbury asks the boy his name, and
upon that information, bases his warring advice:

> Sals.: Sirrah, what's thy name?
> Peter: Peter, forsooth.
> Sals.: Peter, what more?
> Peter: Thump.
> Sals.: Thump? Then see thou thump thy master well.
>
> (2.3.81–84)

Just as Shakespeare used naming to heighten the comedy of his writings, Joyce, too, takes advantage of a system of poetics that would as-
cribe character behavior to names and vice versa; thus, Shakespeare
creates an armorer's apprentice who "thumps" out a living in the workshop, names him *Thump,* and encourages him to "thump" his way to
victory. Joyce names characters in the same spirit, writing into his fiction a multitude of characters who are named ironically or appropriately, comically or seriously, inscribing from *Stephen Hero* through *Finnegans Wake* a nominal tomfoolery that is at once comical and grotesque,
serious and discerning. Each of his characters thumps out an existence,
forging, as in the workshop of Daedalus, a symmetry between himself
and the legacy of his or her name. Making a serious attempt to inscribe
the process by which names are given, handed down, altered, misspelled, and forgotten, Joyce names, unnames, and renames characters to corroborate what, in nature, is our onomastic obsession.

NOTES

WORKS CITED

INDEX

NOTES

1. Joyce also uses *nomen* one other time in the *Wake* as a further pun on Odysseus's "Noman": "he has given to me my necknamesh (flister it!) which is second fiddler to nomen" (*FW* 546.3–4), a nickname (necknamesh) always being second fiddler to a given name or *nomen*.

2. See, for example, Weldon Thornton's "The Allusive Method in *Ulysses*;" in *Approaches to "Ulysses": Ten Essays*.

3. Adaline Glasheen's three censuses of *Finnegans Wake* and Shari and Bernard Benstock's *Who's He When He's at Home* and "Who's He When Who Else Is at Home?"

CHAPTER 1. NAMING AND ALLUSION IN JOYCE

1. See, for example, these references in *Ulysses*: "groatsworth of *mou en civet*" (3.177); "A deathsman of the soul Robert Greene called him" (9.130); "He had a good groatsworth of wit" (9.245); "dearer than his glory of greatest shakescene in the country" (9.926–27); "Where is your brother? Apothecaries' hall. My whetstone" (9.977) (Thornton explains the "whetstone" allusion in reference to Groatsworth in *Allusions in "Ulysses"* 209); "Only crows, priests and English coal are black" (9.1156)—an insightful jibe by Buck Mulligan; I take it as a reference to the "upstart Crow" passage in *Groatsworth of Witte* and argue that Mulligan's assessment of Stephen is an artistic and aesthetic one, and that in his comparison of Stephen's dress with Synge's and Yeats's (a mention of Lady Gregory is also neatly worked in), he is, in fact, comparing the artists' methods, not their attire. A few pages earlier, Mulligan reads aloud the telegram "cribbed out of Meredith," and while the reader cannot be sure whether Mulligan recognizes the "cribbed" quotation or not, since Stephen may be the one thinking those lines in Oxen (*U* 14.1486–1488), his reference to Stephen as a crow suggests that he does, particularly since Shakespeare crows upon his own arrival in Circe, as we shall see; "Whetstone!" (15.2101); and "SHAKE-SPEARE . . . (*he crows with a black capon's laugh*)" (15.3829).

2. Such coats of arms are known as "canting" arms, and a number of literary figures have emblematized their names in such a way. The name *Kafka*, for example, when spelled as *Kavka* with a *v*, is a Czech noun meaning "jackdaw."

The Kafka family was no doubt aware of the serendipitous homonymic "other" meaning of their name because the guild sign hanging in front of Kafka's father's store depicted a black bird.

3. T. S. Eliot, "Phillip Massinger," *The Sacred Wood*, 125.

4. In a letter to Harriet Shaw Weaver on 31 May 1927, Joyce defended himself against numerous claims that he was imitating Lewis Carroll: "I never read him until Mrs Nutting gave me a book, not *Alice*, a few weeks ago—though, of course, I heard bits and scraps. But then I never read Rabelais either though nobody will believe this" (*Letters* 1:255). James Atherton contends that the book Mrs. Nutting probably gave Joyce was Carroll's *Sylvie and Bruno* (127).

5. Joyce also used the word in its sexual sense in letters to Nora, see 8 December 1909, for an early example: "Sometime too I shall surprise you asleep, lift up your skirts and open your hot drawers gently, then lie down gently by you and begin to lick lazily round your bush" (*SL* 185).

6. MacLysaght identifies *Smith* as "the commonest surname in England" (22), and specifies that the name ranks high in Ireland as well, according to R. E. Matheson's study, "Special Report on Surnames in Ireland" (Dublin, 1909), where he lists *Smith* fifth in incidence, MacLysaght reports. In fact, Virginia Woolf comments on the prevalence of the name in *Mrs. Dalloway*: "London has swallowed up many millions of young men called Smith; thought nothing of fantastic Christian names like Septimus with which their parents have thought to distinguish them" (127). Another writer who uses the name *Smith* ironically and to his advantage is Tennessee Williams in *A Streetcar Named Desire*, where the names of the characters are indications of their commonality. Leonard Ashley explains, "Those who can connect *Stella* with 'star' and *Blanche* with 'white' will probably not know Stanley Kowalski's surname means 'smith' in Polish" ("Mudpies" 15).

7. Peter Sims discusses pockets in *Ulysses*, describing the contents of Murphy's pockets in relation to his status as "enemy" in the chapter (250–51).

8. *Henry Flower* was also the name of a D.M.P. constable tried for the murder of Bridget Gannon in 1900. Joyce may have wanted to exploit the suggestiveness of the name, since the trial was such a popular one in the daily press (Garvin 53–57).

CHAPTER 2. NAMING AND HISTORY

1. Cheryl Herr, *Joyce's Anatomy of Culture* (Urbana: University of Illinois Press, 1986); Mary Lowe-Evans, *The Crime against Fecundity: Population Control in the Works of James Joyce* (Syracuse, N.Y.: Syracuse University Press, 1989); see also the *James Joyce Quarterly* issue devoted to Joyce and History (28.4 [1991]).

2. Paul Auster takes the name *Solomon* even further in his novel *Moon Palace* (1989):

> The others around the house called him Solly. He did not object to this nickname, for it somehow left his real name intact, as though it were a secret known only to him: Solomon, the wise king of the Hebrews, a man so precise in his judgments that he could threaten to cut a baby in half. Later on, the diminutive was dropped, and he became Sol. The Elizabethan poets taught him that this was an old word for "sun," and not long after that he discovered it was also the French word for "ground." It intrigued him that he could be both the sun and the earth at the same time, and for several years, he took it to mean that he alone was able to encompass all the contradictions of the universe. (251)

3. *Barnacle* appears in the following passages, all of which might be read as references to Nora, especially the last two: "Man becomes fish becomes barnacle goose becomes featherbed mountain" (*U* 3.478); "*Birds of prey, winging from the sea, rising from marshlands, swooping from eyries, hover screaming, gannets, cormorants, vultures, goshawks, climbing woodcocks, peregrines, merlins, blackgrouse, sea eagles, gulls, albatrosses, barnacle geese*" (*U* 15.4665–4669); "*Yerra, why would she bide with Sig Sloomysides or the grogram grey barnacle gander?* (*FW* 399.10–11); and "He was grey at three, like syngus the swan, when he made his boo to the public and barnacled up to the eyes when he repented after seven" (*FW* 423.21–23).

4. For a sampling, see these in Ithaca: 17.622–23, 17.953, 17.1637, 17.1796, and 17.1873.

5. Not coincidentally, Stephen makes an identical connection in Scylla and Charybdis when he pauses during his paternity lecture to wonder, "Am I a father? If I were? Shrunken uncertain hand" (9.860–61). The similarity of reference in both Bloom's and Stephen's thoughts about masturbation and paternity is further complicated in terms of literary creation, a topic that occupies in varying degrees of seriousness the minds of the two protagonists, since it is an act of the hand that unlike masturbation produces "offspring." Tied, then, to procreation and paternity, literary creation is an avenue to progeny of the invented kind.

6. I quote the remainder of Shoumatoff's litany because it is so unsettling:

> The earthquake of 1906 destroyed most of the birth and marriage records in San Francisco, enabling some Chinese immigrants to claim citizenship as native-born Americans. During the bombing of Exeter in the Second World War, all the wills from southwestern England, which had been gathered there for safekeeping, were destroyed. Professor Lo Hsiang-lin, who had built up in Canton a priceless collection of gazetteers and clan genealogies, which he was forced to leave behind when he fled to Hong Kong from the Communist takeover, later heard from a friend that his collection had appeared in a bookstore which, unable to find another market, had sold them to a grocer for wrapping paper. (250)

Of course, record loss is not the real problem, Shoumatoff is quick to point out, since most of the human population was never recorded to begin with. The loss of documentation is regrettable nonetheless.

7. See Solomon, especially 218–19, where he invokes Ulick O'Connor's description of the incident in his biography of Gogarty.

CHAPTER 3. NAMING AND GENDER

1. The same might be said of male surnames, since they identify sons in terms of their fathers. Patrick McGee treats this issue skillfully in an extended discussion of naming in Scylla and Charybdis (37–68).

2. "Pull down the blinds, love," is also the refrain of a popular music hall song, one Molly most likely would have known.

3. Lady Bloom; Madame Marion Tweedy; Marion of the bountiful bosoms; S. Marion Calpensis; Mrs. Marion; Our Lady of the Cherries; Smutty Moll; Venus Metempsychosis. She is also compared with Gea Tellus. Some of the names characterize Molly as a voluptuous seductress while other names identify her as saint and goddess.

4. In Langston Hughes's poem "Madam's Past History," the speaker notes "My name is Johnson— / Madam Alberta K. / The Madam stands for business. / I'm smart that way" (650).

5. The name *Devlin* is related to "Duibh-linn" (=Dublin). See P. W. Joyce, *The Origin and History of Irish Names of Places*, 1:363. Thomas E. Connolly, in his catalogue of the personal library of Joyce, part of which is contained in the Poetry Collection of the Lockwood Memorial Library at SUNY–Buffalo, notes that Joyce owned an annotated copy of *Irish Names of Places*.

6. *Ni Houlihan* means "daughter of Houlihan." Since the prefixes *O'* and *Mac* denote males, the prefixes are changed to *Ni* and *Nic*, respectively, in the surnames of unmarried females—both *Ni* and *Nic* mean "daughter of." G. B. Adams explains the distinction in his "Prolegomena to the Study of Surnames in Ireland" (89). Even if he hadn't known it already, Joyce would have known from the last line of Yeats's poem "Red Hanrahan's Song About Ireland" that *ni Houlihan* means the daughter of Houlihan.

Joyce wrote "A Mother" in September 1905, just three years after Yeats's legendary production of his play *Cathleen ni Houlihan*. Moreover, in August 1904, a year before he wrote "A Mother," Joyce signed a copy of the song "The Salley Gardens" to Nora with the signature "W. B. Yeats" (R. Ellmann 159).

7. An interesting exception would be instances of self-naming that allow women greater access and more power in the male world, self-chosen *male* names such as *George Eliot*, *George Sand*, and *Acton*, *Currer*, and *Ellis Bell*, for example. Here, the name becomes a mask that hides the woman's gender.

Instead of celebrating the female, as so many of the women's self-generated names do, women's self-chosen male names act like the pseudonymous drapery Fritz Senn alludes to in his essay on naming in *Dubliners*.

8. Eveline's fascination with Frank is much like Desdemona's fascination with Othello; indeed, both Desdemona and Eveline are wooed in Homeric storytelling fashion: "She lov'd me for the dangers I had pass'd, / And I lov'd her that she did pity them," Othello explains to the Duke (*Othello* 1.3.167–68)

9. See Feshbach, " 'Fallen on His Feet in Buenos Ayres,' " and Kenner, *Dublin's Joyce*, 54–55; *The Pound Era*, 34–37; "Molly's Masterstroke," 20–21.

10. Patrick McCarthy points out that this might be a serious question, in that Florence Walzl has shown that the cake Maria asks for is a traditional wedding cake in Ireland. Of course, Maria could be buying the plumcake for someone else, but the girl behind the counter impatiently asks "was it wedding-cake she wanted to buy" before Maria even indicates her desire for plumcake. We are told that because the plumcake in Downes' had too little almond icing on top, Maria "went over to a shop in Henry Street. Here she was a long time in suiting herself and the stylish young lady behind the counter, who was evidently a little annoyed by her, asked her was it wedding-cake she wanted to buy" (*D* 102). As I read this passage, the counter girl's inquiry is spoken rudely and is meant to bully Maria into making a quick purchase.

11. The link may be a sexual one, too, since religious fervor is often described in sexual terms. Exploiting the sexual connection and its unavoidable associations, Joyce irreverently transforms the name *Blessed Margaret Mary Alacoque* into *Blessed Margaret Mary Anycock* in *Ulysses* when Mulligan interrupts Stephen's lecture using the newly rendered name as an expletive (9.646).

CHAPTER 4. NAMING, NAMEPLAY, AND REVENGE

1. One of the groups of names in Scylla and Charybdis is particularly intriguing, albeit troublesome—Stephen's list of the "brood of mockers": "Photius, pseudo Malachi, Johann Most" (9.492). Two of the three names echo the first names of two of Stephen's audience members, Mulligan and Eglinton; but the names cannot be unquestionably attributed to them, since Stephen's "brood of mockers" recalls an earlier list in Telemachus:

> A horde of heresies fleeing with mitres awry: Photius and the brood of mockers of whom Mulligan was one, and Arius, warring his life long upon the consubstantiality of the Son with the Father, and Valentine, spurning Christ's terrene body, and the subtle African heresiarch Sabellius who held that the Father was Himself His own Son. (1.656–60)

In Telemachus, Stephen realizes that he and Mulligan are irreverent Catholics, but since Stephen questions the Church on an intellectual and dogmatic level, instead of on a flippant and satirical level as Mulligan does, Stephen sees himself as a *superior* heretic. He sees Mulligan not as a heretic but as a mocker.

When Mulligan bursts in upon his Shakespeare lecture, trying repeatedly and unsuccessfully to steal the limelight, Stephen recalls his earlier assessment of Mulligan as "mocker" and generates another incriminating list. The later list is not a list of heretics, though; rather, it is a list of false prophets, an office not quite so damaging or execrable.

2. The twins were named after Shakespeare's friends Hamnet and Judith Sadler (Palmer 198, 219).

3. Ferris notes that Joyce consulted Gogarty about syphilis as early as February 1904. On [13 February 1904], Gogarty wrote to Joyce, "Let me hear about your dingus," and in an apparent response to Joyce's letter, Gogarty returned with the following on 10 March 1904, saying, "Congratulations that our holy mother has judged you worthy of the stigmata." Later, on 3 June 1904, Joyce wrote to Gogarty, saying, "Ellwood is nearly cured. I have a rendez-vous with Annie Langton" (*Letters* 1.54). In a subsequent letter from Gogarty, dated 11 June 1904, Gogarty heartily embraces the nominal play and asks Joyce, "How's Elwood?" ("Untold Biography" 7).

Though clearly a reference to Joyce's penis and its syphilitic condition (see Ferris's *James Joyce and the Burden of Disease*), the name *Ellwood* is likely an irreverent allusion to John Ellwood, a medical student who liked to pal around Dublin with Joyce and Gogarty. Stanislaus wrote to Joyce in July 1905 about John Ellwood saying, "Ellwood is capital. He admires your satire very much but says he can hardly think you are not malicious sometimes. He says he would not like to be Gogarty when you come to the Tower episode" (*Letters* 2.103).

CHAPTER 5. NAMING AND IDENTITY

1. Peter Costello notes that thirteen of the names Joyce gave to Stephen's Clongowes mates were "real enough"—*Kickham, Roche, Thunder,* for example—although Joyce "carried away no friendships from Clongowes," and "had no real pal to go around with" (85, 79).

2. Robert Miltner, "The Self-Parody of the Plums," unpublished essay.

WORKS CITED

Adams, G. B. "Prolegomena to the Study of Surnames in Ireland." *Nomina* 3 (1979): 81–94.

Adams, Robert M. *Surface and Symbol: The Consistency of James Joyce's "Ulysses."* New York: Oxford University Press, 1962.

Algeo, John. *On Defining the Proper Name.* Gainesville: University of Florida Press, 1973.

Ashley, Leonard R. N. *What's in a Name?* Baltimore: Genealogical Publishing Company, 1989.

Ashley, Leonard R. N. "Mudpies Which Endure: Onomastics as a Tool of Literary Criticism." In *Names in Literature, Essays from Literary Onomastics Studies,* edited by Grace Alvarez-Altman and Frederick Burelbach, 11–34. Lanham, Md.: University Press of America, 1987.

Atherton, James S. *The Books at the Wake: A Study of Literary Allusions in James Joyce's "Finnegans Wake."* Mamaroneck, N.Y.: Paul P. Appel, 1974.

Atkinson, Frank. *Dictionary of Literary Pseudonyms: A Selection of Popular Modern Writers in English.* 3d ed. London: Clive Bingley, 1982.

Auster, Paul. *Moon Palace.* New York: Penguin Books, 1989.

Barnes, Djuna. *Nightwood.* New York: New Directions, 1937.

Barthes, Roland. "Proust and Names." In *Writing Degree Zero: New Critical Essays,* translated by Richard Howard, 55–68. New York: Hill and Wang, 1980.

Beckett, Samuel. *Three Novels: "Molloy," "Malone Dies," and "The Unnamable."* New York: Grove Press, 1965.

Bell, Robert H. *Jocoserious Joyce: The Fate of Folly in "Ulysses."* Ithaca, N.Y.: Cornell University Press, 1991.

Benstock, Bernard. *James Joyce.* New York: Frederick Ungar, 1985.

Benstock, Shari, and Bernard Benstock. *Who's He When He's at Home: A James Joyce Directory.* Urbana: University of Illinois Press, 1980.

Benstock, Shari and Bernard. "Who's He When Who Else Is at Home?" *James Joyce Literary Supplement* 2.1 (May 1988): 2.

Bishop, John. *Joyce's Book of the Dark: "Finnegans Wake."* Madison: University of Wisconsin Press, 1986.

Black, George F. *The Surnames of Scotland.* New York: New York Public Library, 1962.

Black, J. Anderson. *Your Irish Ancestors.* New York: Paddington Press, 1974.

Borodin, David. " 'Group drinkards maaks grope thinkards or how reads rotary' (FW 312.31): *Finnegans Wake* and the Group Reading Experience." In

"Finnegans Wake": A Casebook, edited by John Harty, 151–64. New York: Garland, 1991.

Bowen, Zack. *"Ulysses."* In *A Companion to Joyce Studies,* edited by Zack Bowen and James Carens, 421–557. Westport, Ct.: Greenwood Press, 1984.

Briffault, Robert. *The Mothers.* London: Allen and Unwin, 1959.

Brown Samuel. *Surnames Are the Fossils of Speech.* N.p., 1967.

Budgen, Frank. *James Joyce and the Making of "Ulysses."* Bloomington: Indiana University Press, 1960.

Burelbach, Frederick M. "An Inquiry into Comic Naming." *Literary Onomastics Studies* 10 (1983): 201–9.

Burelbach, Frederick M. "An Introduction to Naming in the Literature of Fantasy." *Literary Onomastics Studies* 9 (1982): 131–48.

Burelbach, Frederick M. "Names as Distance Controllers in Literature." *Literary Onomastics Studies* 13 (1986): 171–82.

Carroll, Lewis. *The Complete Works of Lewis Carroll.* New York: Random House, 1976.

Cheng, Vincent John. *Shakespeare and Joyce: A Study of "Finnegans Wake."* University Park: Pennsylvania State University Press, 1984.

Cohen, Susan D. "An Onomastic Double Bind: Colette's *Gigi* and the Politics of Naming." *PMLA* 100.5 (1985): 793–809.

Connolly, Thomas E., ed. *The Personal Library of James Joyce: A Descriptive Bibliography.* University of Buffalo Studies, vol. 22, no. 1. Buffalo, N.Y.: University of Buffalo Press, 1955.

Cornog, Martha, and Timothy Perper. "Review: *Deer Man Has the Antlers to Your Questions." Names* 38.4 (Dec. 1990): 375–79.

Costello, Peter. *James Joyce, The Years of Growth: 1882–1915.* West Cork: Roberts Rinehart, 1992.

Culler, Jonathan. "The Call of the Phoneme: Introduction." In *On Puns: The Foundations of Letters,* 1–16. Oxford: Basil Blackwell, 1988.

Derrida, Jacques. *Glas.* Paris: Galilee, 1974.

Des Pres, Terrence. *Praises and Dispraises: Poetry and Politics, the Twentieth Century.* New York: Viking Press, 1988.

Dolch, Martin. "Eveline." In *James Joyce's "Dubliners": A Critical Handbook.* Edited by James R. Baker and Thomas F. Staley, 96–101. Belmont, Cal.: Wadsworth, 1969.

Eliot, T. S. *The Sacred Wood: Essays on Poetry and Criticism.* New York: Methuen, 1983.

Ellmann, Maud. "Polytropic Man: Paternity, Identity and Naming in *The Odyssey* and *Portrait."* In *James Joyce: New Perspectives,* edited by Colin MacCabe, 73–104. Bloomington: Indiana University Press, 1982.

Ellmann, Richard. *James Joyce.* Rev. ed. New York: Oxford University Press, 1982.

Epstein, Edmund L. "Joyce's Names." In *A Companion to Joyce Studies,* edited by

Zack R. Bowen and James F. Carens, 781–82. Westport, Ct.: Greenwood Press, 1984.

Ferrer, Daniel. "Characters in *Ulysses:* 'The Featureful Perfection of Imperfection.' " In *James Joyce: The Augmented Ninth,* edited by Bernard Benstock, 148–51. Syracuse, N.Y.: Syracuse University Press, 1988.

Ferris, Kathleen. *James Joyce and the Burden of Disease.* Lexington: University Press of Kentucky, 1994.

Ferris, Kathleen. "Joyce's Untold Biography." *James Joyce Literary Supplement* 7.1 (Spring 1993): 6–8.

Feshbach, Sidney. " 'Fallen on His Feet in Buenos Ayres': Frank in 'Eveline.' " *James Joyce Quarterly* 20.2 (Winter 1983): 223–27.

Fitch, Noel Riley. "The First *Ulysses.*" In *James Joyce: The Augmented Ninth,* edited by Bernard Benstock, 349–61. Syracuse, N.Y.: Syracuse University Press, 1988.

Fitzgerald, F. Scott. *The Great Gatsby.* 1925. New York: Charles Scribner's Sons, 1980.

Frazer, Sir James George. *The Golden Bough: The Roots of Religion and Folklore.* New York: Avenel Books, 1981.

Frazer, Sir James George. *The Golden Bough: A Study in Magic and Religion.* Abridged edition. New York: Macmillan, 1947.

Freud, Sigmund. *The Complete Psychological Works of Sigmund Freud.* Vol. 6, *The Psychopathology of Everyday Life;* vol. 8, *Jokes and Their Relation to the Unconscious.* Edited by James Strachey *et al.* London: Hogarth Press, 1968.

Friedman, Alan J. "*Ulysses* and Modern Science." *The Seventh of Joyce,* edited by Bernard Benstock, 198–206. Bloomington: Indiana University Press, 1982.

Fussell, Paul. *The Great War and Modern Memory.* London: Oxford University Press, 1977.

Garvin, John. *Joyce's Disunited Kingdom and the Irish Dimension.* London: Gill and MacMillan, 1976.

Gifford, Don. *Joyce Annotated: Notes for "Dubliners" and "A Portrait of the Artist as a Young Man."* Berkeley: University of California Press, 1982.

Gifford, Don, with Robert J. Seidman. *"Ulysses" Annotated: Notes for James Joyce's "Ulysses."* 1974. Berkeley: University of California Press, 1989.

Glasheen, Adaline. *A Second Census of "Finnegans Wake."* Evanston, Ill.: Northwestern University Press, 1963.

Glasheen, Adaline. *A Third Census of "Finnegans Wake."* Berkeley: University of California Press, 1977.

Gleick, James. *Chaos.* New York: Penguin Books, 1987.

Gogarty, Oliver St. J. *As I Was Going down Sackville Street: A Phantasy in Fact.* New York: Reynal and Hitchcock, 1937.

Gogarty, Oliver St. J. Letters. The Rare and Manuscript Collections, Cornell University Library, Ithaca, N.Y.

Greene, Robert. *Facsimile of "Groatsworth of Witte."* New York: Barnes and Noble, 1966.

Groden, Michael. *"Ulysses" in Progress.* Princeton, N.J.: Princeton University Press, 1977.

H D [Hilda Doolittle]. *By Avon River.* New York: Macmillan, 1949.

Harder, Kelsie B. "The Masculine Imperative: Naming by Gael Greene and Erica Jong." *Literary Onomastics Studies* 11 (1984): 147–63.

Harris, Wendell V. "Adam Naming the Animals: Language, Contexts and Meaning." *Kenyon Review* 8.1 (1986): 1–13.

Hart, Clive. *Structure and Motif in "Finnegans Wake."* Evanston, Ill.: Northwestern University Press, 1962.

Hart, Clive and Leo Knuth. *A Topographical Guide to James Joyce's "Ulysses."* Colchester: Wake Newslitter Press, 1981.

Hassan, Ihab. *The Postmodern Turn: Essays in Postmodern Theory and Culture.* Columbus: Ohio State University Press, 1987.

Henke, Suzette, and Elaine Unkeless, eds. *Women in Joyce.* Urbana: University of Illinois Press, 1982.

Herr, Cheryl. *Joyce's Anatomy of Culture.* Urbana: University of Illinois Press, 1986.

Hughes, Langston. "Madam's Past History." In *The Norton Anthology of Modern Poetry.* 2d ed. Edited by Richard Ellmann and Robert O'Clair, 650–51. New York: W. W. Norton, 1988.

Hyman, Louis. *The Jews of Ireland: From the Earliest Times to the Year 1910.* Shannon: Irish University Press, 1972.

Joyce, James. *A Portrait of the Artist as a Young Man.* 1916. New York: Viking Press, 1982.

Joyce, James. *Dubliners.* 1914. New York: Viking Press, 1982.

Joyce, James. *Exiles.* 1918. London: Penguin Books, 1979.

Joyce, James. *Finnegans Wake.* 1939. New York: Viking Press, 1982.

Joyce, James. *Giacomo Joyce.* London: Faber and Faber, 1968.

Joyce, James. *Letters.* Vol. 1, edited by Stuart Gilbert; vols. 2 and 3, edited by Richard Ellmann. New York: Viking Press, 1966.

Joyce, James. *Selected Letters.* Edited by Richard Ellmann. New York: Viking Press. 1975.

Joyce, James. *Ulysses.* 1922. The corrected text, edited by Hans Walter Gabler. New York: Random House, 1986.

Joyce, Patrick Weston. *The Origin and History of Irish Names of Places.* 3 vols. London: Longmans, 1898–1913.

Joyce, Stanislaus. *The Dublin Diary of Stanislaus Joyce.* Ithaca, N.Y.: Cornell University Press, 1962.

Joyce, Stanislaus. *My Brother's Keeper: James Joyce's Early Years.* Edited by Richard Ellmann. New York: Viking Press, 1958.

Jung, Carl G. *The Collected Works of C. G. Jung.* Vol. 8, edited by Herbert Edward Read *et al.* New York: Pantheon Books, 1966.

Kenner, Hugh. *Dublin's Joyce.* Bloomington: Indiana University Press, 1956.

Kenner, Hugh. *The Pound Era.* Berkeley: University of California Press, 1971.

Kenner Hugh. "Molly's Masterstroke." *James Joyce Quarterly* 10.1 (Fall 1972): 19–28.

Lass, Abraham H., David Kiremidjian, and Ruth M. Goldstein. *Dictionary of Classical, Biblical, and Literary Allusions.* New York: Facts on File Publications, 1987.

Lawrence, Karen. "Paternity as Legal Fiction in *Ulysses.*" In *James Joyce: The Augmented Ninth,* edited by Bernard Benstock, 233–43. Syracuse, N.Y.: Syracuse University Press, 1988.

Lawson, E. D. "Men's First Names, Nicknames, and Short Names: A Semantic Differential Analysis." *Names* 21 (1973): 22–27.

Litz, A. Walton. *The Art of James Joyce.* London: Oxford University Press, 1961.

Lowe-Evans, Mary. *The Crime against Fecundity: Population Control in the Works of James Joyce.* Syracuse, N.Y.: Syracuse University Press, 1989.

Macaulay, Thomas Babington. "History." In *Critical and Miscellaneous Essays,* 145–87. Philadelphia: Carey and Hart, 1841.

McCarthy, Patrick A. "The Moore-Joyce Nexus: An Irish Literary Comedy." In *George Moore in Perspective,* edited by Janet E. Dunleavy, 99–116. Gerrards Cross: Colin Smythe, 1983.

McCarthy, Patrick A. *The Riddles of "Finnegans Wake."* Cranbury, N.J.: Associated University Presses, 1980.

McCarthy, Patrick A. *"Ulysses": Portals of Discovery.* Boston: Twayne Publishers, 1990.

McGee, Patrick. *Paperspace: Style as Ideology in Joyce's "Ulysses."* Lincoln: University of Nebraska Press, 1988.

McHugh, Roland. *Annotations to "Finnegans Wake."* London: Routledge and Kegan Paul, 1980.

MacLysaght, Edward. *Irish Families: Their Names, Arms and Origins.* Dublin: Hodges Figgis, 1957.

Maddox, Brenda. *Nora: The Real Life of Molly Bloom.* Boston: Houghton Mifflin, 1988.

Manganiello, Dominic. "Irish Family Names in *Finnegans Wake.*" *A Wake Newslitter* 16 (1979): 30–31.

Matthews, James H. "History to Literature: Alternatives to History in Modern Irish Literature." In *Literature and History,* edited by I. E. Cadenhead, Jr., 73–87. Tulsa: University of Tulsa Monographs, 1970.

Maurer, Warren R. "Trends in Literary Scholarship: German Literary Onomastics: An Overview." *German Quarterly* 56.1 (1983): 89–105.

Michels, James. " 'Scylla and Charybdis': Revenge in James Joyce's *Ulysses.*" *James Joyce Quarterly* 20.2 (Winter 1983): 175–92.

Miller, Casey, and Kate Swift. "Beginning with Names." In *Words and Women: New Language in New Times,* 1–16. Garden City, N.Y.: Anchor Press/Doubleday, 1977.

Millin, Joseph. "Beyond the Uncertainty Principle: Chaos as Clue in *Ulysses*." Unpublished essay.

Miltner, Robert. "The Self-Parody of the Plums." Unpublished essay.

Nadel, Ira B. *Joyce and the Jews: Culture and Texts*. Iowa City: University of Iowa Press, 1989.

O'Brien, Flann. "A Bash in the Tunnel." *Irish Literature: A Reader*. Edited by Maureen O'Rourke Murphy and James MacKillop, 322–27. Syracuse, N.Y.: Syracuse University Press, 1987.

Orr, Linda. "The Revenge of Literature: A History of History." *New Literary History: A Journal of Theory and Interpretation* 18.1 (1986): 1–22.

O'Shea, Michael J. *James Joyce and Heraldry*. Albany: State University of New York Press, 1986.

Oxford English Dictionary. Oxford: Oxford University Press, 1988.

Palme, Andreas. *Die Personennamen im "Ulysses": Eine Studie zur literarischen Onomasatik bei James Joyce*. Erlangen: Palm and Enke, 1990.

Palmer, Alan, and Veronica Palmer. *Who's Who in Shakespeare's England*. New York: St. Martin's Press, 1981.

Partridge, Eric. *Dictionary of Slang and Unconventional English*. 8th ed., edited by Paul Beale. New York: Macmillan, 1984.

Pound, Ezra. *The Literary Essays of Ezra Pound*. Edited by T. S. Eliot. New York: New Directions, 1968.

Ragussis, Michael. *Acts of Naming: The Family Plot in Fiction*. New York: Oxford University Press, 1986.

Reaney, P. H. *A Dictionary of British Surnames*. London: Routledge Kegan Paul, 1958.

Rhys, Jean. *Good Morning, Midnight*. New York: W. W. Norton, 1986.

Riquelme, John Paul. *Teller and Tale in Joyce's Fiction: Oscillating Perspectives*. Baltimore: Johns Hopkins University Press, 1983.

Scholes, Robert. "*Ulysses*: A Structuralist Perspective." *James Joyce Quarterly* 10 (1973): 161–71.

Seed, David. "Naming in Pynchon and Joyce." In *James Joyce: The Centennial Symposium*, edited by Morris Beja *et al.*, 47–56. Urbana: University of Illinois Press, 1986.

Seeman, Mary V. "Name and Identity." *Canadian Journal of Psychiatry* 25 (1980): 129–37.

Seeman, Mary V. "The Unconscious Meaning of Personal Names." *Names* 31 (1983): 237–44.

Senn, Fritz. "Naming in *Dubliners* (a first methermeneutic fumbling)." *James Joyce Quarterly* 24.4 (Summer 1987): 465–68.

Senn, Fritz. "Trivia Ulysseana IV." *James Joyce Quarterly* 19.2 (Winter 1982): 151–78.

Shakespeare, William. *Hamlet*. Edited by Edward Hubler. New York: New American Library, 1963.

Shakespeare, William. *2 Henry VI*. Edited by Milton Crane. New York: New American Library, 1965.

Shakespeare, William. *Othello*. Edited by George Kittredge. Waltham, Ma.: Blaisdell Publishing, 1966.

Shoumatoff, Alex. *The Mountain of Names: A History of the Human Family*. New York: Simon and Schuster, 1985.

Sims, Peter. "A Pocket Guide to *Ulysses*." *James Joyce Quarterly* 26.2 (Winter 1989): 239–58.

Snead, James A. "Some Prefatory Remarks on Character in Joyce." In *James Joyce: The Augmented Ninth*, edited by Bernard Benstock, 139–47. Syracuse, N.Y.: Syracuse University Press, 1988.

Solomon, Albert. "A Moore in *Ulysses*." *James Joyce Quarterly* 10.2 (Winter 1973): 215–27.

Spenser, Edmund. "A Vewe of the Present State of Irelande." *Spenser's Prose Works*, Variorum edition, edited by Rudolf Gottfried. Baltimore: Johns Hopkins University Press, 1949.

Stannard, Una. "Manners Make Laws: Married Women's Names in the United States." *Names* 32 (1984): 114–28.

Stoppard, Tom. *Jumpers*. New York: Grove Press, 1972.

Thomas, Brook. *"Ulysses," A Book of Many Happy Returns*. Baton Rouge: Louisiana State University Press, 1982.

Thom's Official Directory of Dublin, 1904.

Thornton, Weldon. *Allusions in "Ulysses": An Annotated List*. Chapel Hill: University of North Carolina Press, 1988.

Thornton, Weldon. "The Allusive Method in *Ulysses*." In *Approaches to "Ulysses": Ten Essays*, edited by Thomas F. Staley and Bernard Benstock, 235–48. Pittsburgh: University of Pittsburgh Press, 1970.

Toynbee, Paget. *Concise Dictionary of Proper Names and Notable Matters in the Works of Dante*. New York: Phaeton Press, 1968.

Vico, Giambattista. *The New Science of Giambattista Vico*. Edited by Thomas Goddard Bergin and Max Harold Fisch. Ithaca, N.Y.: Cornell University Press, 1991.

Walker, Emery R. "An Aptonym A Day. . . ." *American Name Society Bulletin* 81 (Apr. 1988): 7.

Wall, Richard. "Buck Mulligan's Revenge: Joyce in the Works of Gogarty." In *Studies in Anglo-Irish Literature*, edited by Heinz Kosok, 89–94. Bonn: Bouvier, 1982.

Woolf, Virginia. *Mrs. Dalloway*. 1925. New York: Harcourt Brace Jovanovich, 1953.

INDEX

Achburn, 40

Adams, Robert, 17

AE (George Russell), 103

Ahasuerus, 96

Alacoque, Blessed Mary Margaret, 93, 133*n11*

Aliases, 25–26

Alice, 30

Aligheri, Dante, 36, 37, 40

Allfours, 121, 122

Anti-Semitism (revealed in naming), 122

Anycock, Margaret Mary, 133*n11*

Aptonyms, 111–13, 116–18

Aquinas, St. Thomas: *Contra Gentiles*, 11

Ashley, Leonard, 3, 5, 27–28, 130*n6*

Ashreborn, 40

Athy, 32, 79, 116

Auden, W. H., 20

Aujey (JJ pseudonym), 104

Auster, Paul: *Moon Palace*, 78–79, 131*n2*

Bardic practices and naming, 95–97

Barnacle, 55, 117, 131*n3*

Barnes, Djuna, 72, 73

Barry, Mrs. Yelverton, 73

Barth, John, 102

Barthes, Roland, 57

Bartoluzzi, 17

Beag, Seamus, 77

Beau Mount and Lecher, 66

Beckett, Samuel: *The Unnamable*, 20, 118

Bell, Robert, 23

Benstock, Bernard, 4, 81

Benstock, Shari, 4

Best, Beautifulinsadness, 95, 103

Best, Best, 103

Best, Richard, 31

Best, Secondbest, 95–96, 103

Besteglinton, 99, 102, 103

Biddy the Clap, 79

Bishop, John, 50, 103

Blavatsky, Madame, 41

Bloom, Leopold, 23, 24, 57, 62, 124

Bloom, Lady, 87, 132*n3*

Bloom, Milly, 30, 77, 79, 113, 119–20

Bloom, Molly, 30, 76–77, 79, 119

Bloom, Mrs. Marion, 85–88, 132*n3*

Blum, 25

Boanerges, 69

Boardman, Edy, 79

Bodkin, 64

Bodley, Bernard, 40–41

Bollopedoom, 40, 124

Boodle, Lord, 102

Boom, L., 40, 123

Borodin, David, 6

Boru, Brian, 35, 56

Boudin, A., 22–23

Bovum, Bos, 41, 62

Bowen, Zack, 98, 100

Boylan, Blazes, 79

Boyle, "Lady," 31

Boyle, Tusker, 31, 79, 118

Breen, Josie, 79

Breen, Mrs. Denis, 73

Browne, 64

142

Buckmulligan, 103
Budgen, Frank, 16, 100
Bullockbefriending bard, 96
Buonoparte, Napolean, 17
Burelbach, Frederick, 101–2
Burke, O'Madden, 88
Burke, Pisser, 79
Burke, Thomas Henry, 46
Bushe, Seymour, 15, 124
Butterfly Effect, the, 44
Byron, Patrick, 19

C___, E___, 94
Caffrey, Cissy, 79
Calpensis, S. Marion, 132n3
Campbell, Foxy, 79
Canting arms, 129n2
Cantwell, 79, 116
Carey, Denis, 80–81
Carey, James, 80–81
Carey, Peter, 80
Carlilse, Lily, 79
Carroll, Lewis, 11, 13, 29–31, 34,
    130n4
Cavalcanti, Guido, 37
Chandler, Annie, 79
Chandler, Little, 104
Chandler, T. Malone (Little Chan-
    dler's pen name), 25, 104, 124
Chanel (JJ pseudonym), 104
Chaos Theory, 44–45
Chauchat, 28
Cheng, Vincent, 83, 100
Cherries, Our Lady of the, 124,
    132n3
Childs Fratricide Case, The, 15
Chin Chon Eg Lin Ton, 103
Christicle, 124
Cicero, 17
Clifford, Martha, 79
Cockburn, 40
Cockshott, J. P., 33, 40

Coffey, Father, 82
Cognomen Syndrome, The, 112–13
Cohen, Susan, 72
Coincidence: of dates, 5, 100; of
    names, 6, 122–23
Colesser, Monico (JJ pseudonym),
    104
Comisky, Bags, 39–40, 79
Conacre, Cowe, 121
Conrad, Borys, 16
Costello, Frank "Punch," 60–61
Costello, Peter, 122, 134n1
Cranly, 35
Cridders, 59–60
Crotthers, 59–60
Crowbar, 14
Culler, Jonathan, 113–14
Curran, C. P., 69
Cursing and blaming, 95, 97

Daedalus, 111, 113, 125
Daedalus, Stephen (JJ pseudonym),
    14, 25, 104
Dalloway, Mrs. Richard (Clarissa),
    75
Defoe, Daniel: *Moll Flanders*, 76
Dedalus, 14, 22, 23, 110, 113
Dedalus girls, The (Boody, Maggy,
    Dilly, Katey), 79
Dedalus, Simon, 22, 113, 124
De Kock, Paul, 40, 76
Denis, 82
Dermot, 69
Derrida, Jacques, 55, 113–14
Des Pres, Terrence, 97
Devlin, 132n5
Dewey-Mosse, Mrs. Kitty, 122
Dickens, Charles: *Bleak House*, 102
Dignam, Patk., 66
Dignam, Susy, 79
Dillon: Floey, Atty and Hetty, 79
Dolan, Fr., 19

Donne, John, 55, 114
Donnelly, Mrs., 73
Dowie, Alexander J. Christ, 66
Dowie, Dr. John Alexander, 66
Doyle, 17–18, 29, 113
Doyle, Jimmy, 18
Doyler, Judge Jeremy, 18
Dubedat, Miss, 121
Dubedatandshedidbedat, Miss 121
Dumbo, 78

Earwicker/Porter, 14, 113
Eclecticon, John, 96, 103
Eglantine, 102
Eglinton, 99
Eglinton, Johannes, 102–3
Eglinton, John sturdy, 102
Eglinton, Judge, 102
Eglinton, littlejohn, 102, 124
Eglinton, Second, 102
Eglinton, ugling, 96, 102
Eglintonus Chronolologos, 102
Einstein, Albert, 44
Eliot, T. S., 13, 38–39, 114
Ellison, Ralph Waldo, 20, 31
Ellmann, Maud, 99
Ellmann, Richard, 97, 104, 112
Ellwood (JJ's pseudonym for penis),
    105, 134n3
Emma, 89
Endymion, 46–49, 67
Eve, 89–90

Farrell, Cashel Boyle O'Connor
    Fitzmaurice Tisdall, 46–49, 67
Farrell, James Boyle Tisdell Burke
    Stewart Fitzsimons, 46–49, 67
Farrington, Ada, 79, 89
Ferrer, Daniel, 118
Ferris, Kathleen, 105, 134n3
Festy King, 14

Figatner, 82, 123
Finnegan, 46
Fitzgerald, 14
Fitzgerald, F. Scott: The Great Gatsby,
    109–10
Fleming, Lizzie, 79
Fleury, Henri 26
Flor, Senhor Enrique, 26
Flower, Henry (Bloom's pseud-
    onym), 25–27, 62, 124, 130
Flynn, Fr., 124
Flynn, Nannie, 79
Flynn, Nosey, 41, 79
Fogg, Marco Stanley, 78
Fogg, Phileas, 78
Fraidrine (Fred Ryan), 98–99
Frank (in "Eveline"), 91–93
Freidman, Alan, 44
Freud: 17, 123; on the forgetting of
    proper names, 82; on jokes, 82
Furey, 64

G. C. (Gabriel Conroy's pen name),
    25
Galway, Tribes of, 64–65
Garry, Owen, 121
Garryowen, 124
Gauguin, Paul, 13
Genet, Jean, 55, 113
Glasheen, Adaline, 4
Glencree Reformatory dinner, the,
    84–86
Glynn, Madame, 87
Godonuv, Boris, 16
Goff, Master, 22
Gogarty, Oliver (character in
    Moore's The Lake), 70
Gogarty, Oliver St. John: 11, 70–71,
    104–5, 106, 107; As I Was Going
    down Sackville Street, 47–48
Goodbody, 17
Goulding, Collis and Ward, 124

Goulding, Sally and Crissie, 79
Grania, 69
Grannuaile, 69
Greaseabloom, 94
Greasy eyes, 94
Greene, Robert: *Groatsworth of Witte*, 8–10, 129*n1*
Gregory, Lady Augusta, 8–10
Griffin, Peggy (see also Martha Clifford), 79
Griffith, Arthur, 49
Groden, Michael, 16
Gygasta, Carpulenta, 32–33

H. D., 114
Hahn, twice Mrs. (nee Hahn-Hahn), 41
Hart, Clive, 48
Hawwah, 89
Hayes, 14
Hayman, David, 98
Healy, Miss, 89
Heisenberg Uncertainty Principle, the, 44–45
Hemingway, Ernest, 114
Henke, Suzette, 93
HERE COMES EVERYBODY, 28–29, 121
Heron, 33–34, 35, 113
Herpyllis, Nell Gwynn, 96
Herr, Cheryl, 102, 130*n2*
Higgins, 24
Hilary, 69
Hill, Ernest, 91–92
Hill, Eveline, 37–38, 91–93. *See also* Poppens *and* Evvy Hill
Hill, Evvy, 79
Holohan, Hoppy, 11, 79, 88–89
Horne, Andrew, 113, 117–18
Hughes, Langston, 132*n4*
Hupinkoff, Boris, 16
Hurhausdirektorpresident, Herr, 16

Iagogo, 83
Iagogogo, 83
Iopas, Hairy, 124
Issy, 89, 113
Ivors, Molly, 79

J. A. A. J., 93
Jack, 21
James, 21
Jerko, 78
Jesus, 17
Jewy, 122
Joe, 21
Joyce, 65
Joyce, Giorgio, 117
Joyce, Lucy/Lucia, 117
Jung, Carl ("yung"), 93, 122–23
Junius, 25, 96
Justice, Beatrice, 36–37, 124

Kafka, Franz, 20, 129–30*n2*
Karoly, 24, 124
Kathleen, 12
Kearney, Kathleen, 11, 88–89
Kelly, Bridie, 79
Kempthorpe, Clive, 39
Kennedy, Jacqueline, 4–5
Kennedy, Mina, 79
Kenner, Hugh, 92
Kernan, Tomgin, 96
Kickham, Rody, 113, 116, 134*n1*
Kinch, 96, 100
Kinch the knifeblade, 79
Knuth, Leo, 48
Kock, Poldy, 40
Kranliberg, 124
Kratinabritchisitch, Goosepond Prhtr, 16

Lacan, Jacques, 75
Lankester, Rose, 71
Lardyface, Old, 96

Laredo, Lunita, 77
Lawrence, Karen, 12
Lily (the caretaker's daughter), 79
Litz, A. Walton, 15
Livingstone, Dr. Stanley, 78
Lovebirch, James, 25
Lowe-Evans, Mary, 80, 130n2
Lynch, 58, 63–65

M'Intosh, 35, 58
MacAnaspey, Mr. and Mrs. Ditto (JJ
    pseudonym), 25, 104
McCarthy, Patrick A., 66, 70, 116,
    133n10
MacDowell, Gerty, 79
Macduff, 96
McGee, Patrick, 100, 132n1
MacGinty (JJ pseudonym), 25, 104
Mackerel, 35, 79, 96
Madame, 86–87
Madden, 22
Maddox, Brenda, 5–6, 104
Magee Mor Matthew, 77
Magee, William Kirkpatrick, 103
Mageeglinjohn, 102, 103
Mahony, 74
Maledicty (Mulligan), 58
Mangan's sister, 118
Mann, Thomas, 28
Marion, 30, 76, 77
Marion of the bountiful bosoms,
    132n3
Marionette, 77
Martha and Mary, 30
Martin, 30
Matthews, James, 43
Meissel, Pimply, 41, 79
Metempsychosis, Venus, 132n3
Michels, James, 101
Millicent, 77
Millin, Joseph, 45
Miltner, Robert, 134n2

Milton, John, 73, 89
Mo, Ikey, 122
Moll, Mrs., 85
Moll, Smutty, 85–86, 132n3
Mooney, Polly, 79
Moore, George, 70
Moran, Fr., 19
Morkan, Kate, 79
Moses/Mosse/Moss, 122
Moses, Ikey, 96, 122
Mulligan, Ballocky, 102, 103
Mulligan, Buck, 79
Mulligan, Cuck, 99, 102, 103
Mulligan, Malachi, 103
Mulligan, Monk, 99, 102, 103
Mulligan, Puck, 102, 103
Mulvey, Lt., 80–81, 123–24
Mumbo Jumbo, 78
Murphy, 3, 14, 17–18, 23, 25, 74

"Nailing a name," 97
Nameless One, The, 118
Names: actual names, 14–16; allu-
    sive names, 1–42; appropriate
    names, 117 (*see also* aptonyms);
    backward names, 6; palindromes,
    89–90; slotting names, 21; sur-
    names, 56, 57; virtue, 91–92
Naming: and allusion, 1–42; and co-
    incidence, 5, 122–23; and cursing,
    97; and determinism, 28–32, 109–
    25; and diminutives, 79–80; as
    drapery, 79, 94, 132–33n7; and for-
    getfulness, 82; and gender, 72–94;
    and history, 43–71; and identity,
    109–28; and jokes, 82; and law, 51;
    and magic, 31, 97; and marriage,
    73, 75; and namelessness, 117; and
    nameplay, 95–108; and pseud-
    onyms, 14, 25–27, 62, 103–5, 124,
    130, 132n6, 134n3; and revenge,
    95–108; and sexuality; 7, 26, 28,

Naming (*continued*)
30, 31, 33, 39–40, 76, 79, 81–82, 85–86, 102, 103, 105, 118, 124, 132*n3*, 133*n11*, 134*n3*; and superstition, 5–6, 31
Nadel, Ira, 24, 55
Navigator, The Impervious (D. B. Murphy), 23
Ni Houlihan, Kathleen, 12, 88–89, 132*n6*

O'Brien, 14
O'Brien, Flann, 20, 106–7
O'Connell, 14
O'Connor, 14
O'Donnell, 14
O'Reilly, Maggot, 79
O'Shea, Michael, 35, 41
O'Shem the Draper, Mr., 74
Old Ollebo, M. P., 40, 124
Opisso, Mrs., 75–76
Orr, Linda, 43
Overman, James (JJ pseudonym), 104

Palme, Andreas, 122
Papli, 94
Parnell, Charles Stewart, 46
Peeter the Picker, 81
Pendennis, 81, 123
Penrose, 81
Peter, uncle, 26, 124
Pickackafax, Peter, 79
Pirandello, Luigi, 20
Pisimbo, Mrs., 75
Plato: *Cratylus* 28
Plurabelle, Anna Livia, 14, 89–91
Podmore, 17
Poldy, 96
Polo, Marco, 78
Polo Shirt, 78
Ponge, Francis, 55, 114

Poppens, 79. *See* Eveline Hill
Porter/Earwicker, 14, 79, 113
Pound, Ezra, 38, 114
Prankquean's Tale, The (naming in), 68–69
Proust, Marcel, 57
Pseudonyms (JJ's) 25, 104, 132*n6*
Pseudonyms, 103–4. *See also* Naming, and pseudonyms
Pulchrabelled, Allaniuvia (ALP), 4
Purefoy: Mamy, Budgy and Mina, 79; Mortimer Edward, 66

Quakerlyster, 83, 99, 103
Quantum theory, 44

Rabworc, 14
Ragussis, Michael, 34, 119, 120
Ramsbottom, 75
Rat rhymers, 97
Ratatuohy, 33
Reephen, 40
Rhys, Jean: *Good Morning, Midnight* 90, 118
Riordan, Dante, 94
Riquelme, John Paul, 93
Rivière, 19
Roche, Nasty, 79, 113, 115, 134*n1*
Ryan, Fred, 98–99
Ryan, 14

Seed, David, 18, 123
Seeman, Mary, 74, 78–79
Ségouin, 19
Senn, Fritz, 74, 122, 132–33*n7*
Sexuality. *See* Naming, and sexuality
Shaggspick, 13
Shakespeare, Edmund, 105, 106
Shakespeare, Gilbert, 105–6
Shakespeare, Patrick, W., 19
Shakespeare, Richard, 105
Shakespeare, William, 8–10, 12–13,

Shakespeare, William (*continued*)
   17–18, 26, 34–35, 39, 55, 83, 100–
   101, 105–6, 125, 129*n1*
Shakhisbeard, 13
Shemoth, 3
Shipahoy (D. B. Murphy), 23
Shirt Face, 78
Shit Face, 78
Shouldrup, 41
Shoumatoff, Alex, 67–68, 131–32*n6*
Simonetti, 17
Sims, Peter, 130*n7*
Sinbad the sailor, etc., 101–2
Sinico, Emily, 12, 73
Sinico, Captain, 12
Sitwell, Edith, 114
Skibbereen father, The (D. B. Mur-
   phy), 23
Smith, 3, 17–18, 25, 74, 130
Snead, James, 95
Solomon, 52, 131*n2*
*Some mote him Mike, some vote him
   Vike . . .* (FW 44.10–14), 49–54, 102
Sonmulligan, 96, 103
Soulpetre, 40
Spenser, Edmund, 52, 95
Squaretoes, Thomas, 79
St. Jesus, O. (Gogarty), 70
Staylewit, 121, 122
Steadfast John, 102
Steeeeeeeeeeeephen, 40
Stein, Gertrude, 114
Stephaneforos, 66, 96
Stephens, James, 6
Stern, Laurence: *Tristram Shandy* 22
Stoppard, Tom: *Jumpers* 112–13
Storiella, 43
Sullivan, 14

Talmud, the, 3
Tandy, Shapland, 22

Tar, Jack (D. B. Murphy), 23
Tarpaulin, The Communicative (D.
   B. Murphy), 23
Teirrah, Revaew (Harriet Weaver), 6
Thermodynamics, second law of, 44
Thom's Directory, 14, 22, 69
Thomas, Brook, 75, 81, 104
Thump, Peter, 125
Thunder, Cecil, 113, 116, 134*n1*
Tittlemouse, Tommy, 96
Tom, 21
Tribes of Galway, the, 64–65
Tristopher, 69
Tuckoo, Babie, 115–16
Tuohy ("Ratatuohy"), 33
Tweedy, 76
Tweedy, Madame Marion, 132*n3*
Tykingfest, 14

Ulysses (JJ pseudonym), 104
Unkeless, Elaine, 93

Vico, Giambatista, 51, 93
Villona, 19
Virag, 24, 124

Wall, Richard, 107
Walsh, 14
Watchman, Minnie, 79
Weaver, Harriet, 5, 6, 67, 130*n4. See
   also* Revaew Teirrah
Wilde, Oscar: *Picture of Dorian Gray*
   10–11
Wolfe, Thomas, 114
Woolf, Virginia: 114; *Mrs. Dalloway*
   75, 130*n6*

Yeats, W. B. (JJ pseudonym), 25,
   104, 132*n6*
Yeats, William Butler, 97, 114
Yorke, Blanche, 71